BACKUP ON THE BEAT

*An Inspiring Collection of Stories, Essays and
Thoughts for America's Peace Officers*

BACKUP
ON THE BEAT

*An Inspiring Collection of Stories, Essays and
Thoughts for America's Peace Officers*

STEPHEN C. LEE, M.DIV.

Pascoe Publishing
Rocklin, California

Cover design by Salmon Associates
Page design by Melanie Haage Design

ISBN: 1-929862-07-5

01 02 03 10 9 8 7 6 5 4 3 2 1

Printed in the United States of America

DEDICATION

THIS BOOK IS DEDICATED TO THE MEMORY OF Sergeant Rick Weinhold, Saint Louis County Police, St. Louis, Missouri. On Tuesday, October 31, 2000, Sgt. Weinhold responded with fellow officers to a disturbance call and, upon arrival, chose to lead from the front. In the subsequent building search, the suspect ambushed Sgt. Weinhold with a shotgun. Although mortally wounded, Rick pushed his fellow officers to safety and returned fire. Previously honored by the State of Missouri as their top academy instructor, Rick was posthumously awarded law enforcement's highest award, the Medal of Honor. Rick was also a friend and ministry partner, who in his life modeled the beliefs and principles discussed in this book. Until we meet again in heaven, he remains in our hearts.

ACKNOWLEDGMENTS

M Y THANKS TO A NUMBER OF PEOPLE WHO, DIRECTLY or indirectly, have helped create this book and have backed me up in life with their wisdom and encouragement. Love to my wife and children, who have walked the journey with me and who love me back, warts and all. A special thanks to my wife, who lovingly helped me research all the verses for this book (I love you, sweetheart—let's do dinner). Love also to my folks, who firmly grasped life's lessons and taught them the best way—by example. Thanks to Karen Pascoe of Pascoe Publishing, who cheerfully provided adult supervision and corralled me from my occasional detours the long way round the barn. Thanks, too, to Mark Cook, whose good taste made Karen's involvement possible. Special thanks to my assistant, Cheryl, who faithfully points me in the right direction and picks up after me. Honor goes to my mentors, Dr. Eugene "Obi-Wan" Bunkowske and the sainted Rev. Theodore Polster, who taught me well from Luther to study and pray through life's testings. Hats off to the Chief, Bob Vernon, who remains The Man. Appreciation to Michael Hackbardt for putting me on the publishing road. Salutes to Dave Neumann, Bob Tassler, Mike Flannery, John South, and Denny Conroy, who have walked with me through the occasional shadowed valley. Salutes also to my long-time friends, Bob and Sue

McMenomey, who provide hideouts, R & R, and steadfastness, and to Steve Austin, fellow gladiator and tilter at windmills. Heartfelt thanks to all the board members, advisors, and constituents of Peace Officer Ministries—too many to name individually—who have contributed to this project and this ministry. Because of your friendship and faithfulness, we continue to have an amazing ride.

Always and ultimately, gratitude to heaven's backup, our peace officer, Jesus Christ. Glory to him alone!

TABLE OF CONTENTS

Introduction	*xi*
The Moment of Truth	*1*
Are You a "Wrong-Way" Driver?	6
A Tiny Corner	*11*
Spiritual "Situational Awareness"	*12*
Can A Cop Be A Christian?	*15*
Your Authority as a Peace Officer	24
Our Backup	26
Profiles in Courage	28
Jesus Christ, the Ultimate Peace Officer	34
My Unseen Partner	35
The Barbed Wire	40
A Question of Integrity	43
If God is A Loving God...	53
A Cop Christmas Carol	62
An Island of Hope	74
Your Weapons on the Spiritual Street	78
Old, New, and Renewed Centurions	79

Drawing the Line   83
A Real Word for a Real World   90
Ten Tips for Spiritual Survival as a Peace Officer   92
Shoot or Don't Shoot   99
Verses to Use in Arresting...   108
"John Wayne" Syndrome   118
The Cop at the Cross   124
Help! I'm Married to a Cop!   132
African Time   141
Hitting the Wall   147
The Five Golden Keys of Stress Management
    for Cops   155
One More   161
The Basics of Belief: Tying It All Together   163
What Legacy Will You Leave?   169

INTRODUCTION

P EACE OFFICERS ARE THE SHEPHERDS WHO STAND
between the sheep and the wolves. If they are to survive
and win in their important vocation, if they are to truly protect and serve, they must always be alert to predators, on
guard against bushwhackers, practiced in tactics, equipped
for battle, strong with integrity, guided by principle, driven by
mission, and grounded in belief.

The vocation of peace officer is fundamentally a calling of
the spirit, based on noble ideals (for example, "to protect and
serve"). No amount of material gain—hummingbird small
anyway—is enough to justify the price officers pay for their
dedication. Officers must *believe* to *achieve*. They must
believe their mission justifies the sweat, the tears, and the
blood they shed, to avoid despair and to achieve purpose and
meaning. They must believe there is a greater good than self-
gratification, because good law enforcement demands self-
sacrifice. Otherwise, they cave in to the worst of all worlds by
burying their heads until retirement, all for the sake of a pid-
dly paycheck, while the wolves devour the sheep.

An officer's calling can be difficult and disillusioning, to
say the least. Despite the propaganda of post-modern human-
istic philosophy, cops know from hard-earned experience the

corrupt reality of the human condition. They understand that people are ultimately incapable of self-improvement and often do not even want to improve. They know that the world *is* going to hell in a hand-basket. Unfortunately, if they lack positive beliefs to address that reality, they are driven to hopelessness and despair. One of the tragic ironies of law enforcement is that the peace officers who bring peace to others often have no peace themselves. This, too, is spiritual reality.

The message of the Christian gospel ("gospel" means "good news") meets the need we all have in life for explanation, hope, guidance, and strength. The biblical message matches cops' observations. The Bible talks about humanity's fall from perfection and the reality of sin and corruption and pain and death. The Bible agrees with an officer's observation that we must look beyond ourselves for answers, because we are not capable or even willing to find life's answers on our own. The Bible lays out straightforward guidelines for finding those answers and gives us hope and strength. This is a real spiritual answer to our real spiritual problem.

The main message of the Bible, which should be easily understood by officers, is that we cannot and must not play "John Wayne" in life. Just like playing John Wayne on the street will get you physically killed, playing John Wayne in your heart will get you spiritually killed.

There were times when I was a cop when I needed help, no matter how well prepared I was. That is why I had a radio. Sometimes I was stupid not to use it. Life off the street is like life on the street. Sometimes we need an equalizer beyond ourselves and our own tools. Sometimes we simply need backup and we would be stupid not to call for it. It amazes me how well some officers understand this principle on the street, but are too stubborn to recognize it in their personal lives and, consequently, lose everything dear to them. They play John Wayne and refuse to call for spiritual backup. However, many officers do recognize their need for backup in their personal lives. These shepherds understand their own need for a shepherd who can protect and serve them and who can heal their lost innocence. These are the officers who survive not just physically, but emotionally, relationally, and spiritually, as well.

This book is intended for spiritual backup. It is an edited and expanded compilation of articles from *The Renewed Centurion*, the monthly periodical of Peace Officer Ministries. I invite you to read the selections here for personal reflection and study and to simply enjoy. This book may also serve as a foundation for group Bible study and discussion. My intent will be happily satisfied if officers here find insight, application, and hope.

These stories and essays, although written in a variety of ways about a variety of subjects, have one ultimate object in mind. They were written to portray our peace officer, Jesus Christ, and to tell you about the help he provides. May this Good Shepherd, who was made the sacrificial Lamb of God to save us all, always back you up on life's beat!

∞

THE MOMENT OF TRUTH

ONE SUMMER DAY I WAS WALRUS-SPRAWLED ON A floating swimming dock, soaking up some California lake rays and letting go of some stress during our family vacation. Just then, my daughter dove into the water and the watch she was wearing slipped from her arm and sank into the depths of the lake. "Don't worry, Dad, it's waterproof," she said, as we peered down into the water. I dove in to retrieve it, but could not dive deep enough to find the bottom, never mind the watch. But, I am a creative soul, not distracted in the slightest by minor concerns like common sense or a fear of drowning. (My stupidity is sometimes of the weighty, proud, pure, shining, unalloyed 24-karat gold variety).

I went to the car and borrowed my son's diving mask. Then, arming myself with a thirty-pound boulder, I navigated my way back to the dock. Being the astute person I am, I figured I could probably achieve better vision with the mask and better depth with the rock. (One of my "wise-guy" cop buddies later mentioned that he was surprised I didn't tie myself to the rock to ensure a successful mission, thus qualifying myself for a Darwin award). I walked to the edge of the dock, pulled the mask onto my face, hoisted the boulder in my arms and, taking a deep breath, jumped into the water.

The boulder exceeded my expectations. It worked really well—better than I had hoped. In fact, I could hardly clear the pressure from my ears during the rock(et) ride down into the deep. I was about twenty or twenty-five feet under the water when I finally spotted the bottom, still a fair distance below. I say, "spotted," because that perfectly describes my vision. The watery vise on my head was causing my eyes to cross and my vision to blur with spots. It briefly occurred to me that I should have brought a flag along to plant on this inverted Mt. Everest, because surely no person had ever set foot on the ground where I was headed. That quick thought was followed by another more urgent message, which suggested that maybe it was time to get my daughter a new watch so that she wouldn't have to wear that old thing anymore and, coincidentally, so that my head would not implode exactly like a politician's reputation.

Fish or cut bait? Drop the boulder or *become* bait?

I could see the bottom, but not the watch, and it was definitely decision time. Fish or cut bait? Drop the boulder or *become* bait? Even a rock(et) scientist like me quickly figured out that, if I wanted to avoid the day of reckoning, I had better recognize the moment of truth. I let go of that boulder and surfaced to shop for a new watch.

I missed out on a Darwin award, but not on another story to enhance my reputation. (I seem to collect these like baseball cards. I have no idea why.) Later that day, my wife was visiting with some nice church ladies who were having a picnic at the lake. When I stopped by to say hello, one of them gave me a skeptical look and then politely said, "Oh, yes, you're the man with the rock..."

It occurs to me that my deep-sea diving experience is a wonderful metaphor for life (with my propensity for trouble, I pick up a lot of metaphors along the way). More than once I have had a *desire* or *goal* (save the watch). This desire or goal may or may not have been a good thing to begin with, but when I *stubbornly clung to pursuing it, no matter what* (the rock), I found myself *sinking*

What desire or goal are you chasing that has you clinging to the rock of unhealthy pursuit in the lake of life?

deeper and deeper into the depths within myself and in my relationship with God and others (the lake). Then came the moment of truth when I realized I would have to let go of pursuing the goal or desire, or suffer the day of reckoning—*losing my hope, my peace, my integrity or my cherished relationships* (drowning).

Unfortunately, there have been times when I found myself tied to the rock of pursuit by the rope of sin, hell-bent southward into the dark depths without a knife, not to find a gold watch, but instead to receive the devil's own Darwin award.

What about you? What desire or goal are you chasing that has you clinging to the rock of unhealthy pursuit in the lake of life? What tempting stone are you unwilling to drop? Let it go, partner, or it will drown you. Don't let your moment of truth turn into your day of reckoning. And, if there is some sin or sorrow that won't let you go, let Jesus cut the rope. After all, he already cut the Gordian knot of our human condition two thousand years ago, when he tied himself to the rock of the cross and willingly drowned—in our place—in the sin and suffering and sorrow of the entire human race. If he can cut that impossible knot for the whole world, he can surely cut it for <u>you</u>.

Dear Father in heaven,
Help me to see and let go of the rocks in my life that are dragging me down into the depths. Help me understand the truth that, by bowing before you, I can stand straight in the world. Thank you for sending your beloved Son as my backup peace officer. I praise you that, by his willing death on the cross, he took the bullet Satan meant for me, and he cut the knot of sin I was unable to untie. I give you glory that, because he rose again, I, too, can have new life. Give me your vision so that I can always focus on him, the source and goal of my faith. Help me to not grow tired and give up, but by your Spirit's strength, may I always have your hope in my heart, so that one day, someday, I can have heaven. In the name of your Son, Jesus Christ, my Savior and Lord, I pray.
Amen.

"O Lord, out of the depths I call to you. O Lord, hear my voice. Let your ears be open to my pleas for mercy. O Lord, who would be able to stand if you kept a record of sins? But with you there is forgiveness so that you can be feared. I wait for the Lord, my soul waits, and with hope I wait for his word. My soul waits for the Lord more than those who watch for the morning, more than those who watch for the morning." *Psalm 130:1-6*

"Since we are surrounded by so many examples of faith, we must get rid of everything that slows us down, especially sin that distracts us. We must run the race that lies ahead of us and never give up. We must focus on Jesus, the source and goal of our faith. He saw the joy ahead of him, so he endured death on the cross and ignored the disgrace it brought him. Then he received the highest position in heaven, the one next to the throne of God. Think about Jesus, who endured opposition from sinners, so that you don't become tired and give up. *Hebrews 12:1-3*

ARE YOU A
"WRONG-WAY" DRIVER?

S CENE DESCRIPTION: SUNDAY, FEBRUARY 15TH, 1135 hrs: Eastbound number one lane on I-70, divided highway (two lanes each direction, separated by about 100 yards of median strip), 5 miles east of the Colorado-Utah border, speed limit 75 miles per hour, partial high clouds, visibility good, road condition dry and clear, traffic light.

My five-year-old daughter was in the back seat of our tin-can sized Geo Metro, with her seat belt on. My wife was dozing next to me in the front passenger seat. I was pushing the speed limit in the Geo's efficient fifth-gear overdrive, thankful that the long return drive from California was nearing its conclusion. Because of snowstorms, we had been forced to take an extra day on the way back. The stress of the previous two days' drive through bad weather had robbed me of the rest the extra overnight would have provided. God had richly blessed our ministry trip to the law enforcement conference at Mount Hermon, California, but now I was tired. I wanted to get home.

At that instant, had I glanced at the beautiful snow-covered scenery, we would have been killed. I had no time to think—

Stephen C. Lee

only react. One moment was calm and beautiful. The next flashed an image of a red compact car cresting the rise immediately in front of me, rushing toward us in our lane. One moment peaceful—the next a deadly game of "Chicken" at a combined closure speed of 150 miles per hour. The two little cars with their assorted passengers were a split-second from disintegration.

But, this time wasn't God's time. I don't really remember turning the wheel, just that we were suddenly in the next lane and the red compact car blew past. I didn't even have time to be scared until it was over. I checked to see if my family was unhurt and, as I fought off the shakes and my growing anger, a fifteen-year-old memory of another deceptively quiet Sunday morning flashed in my mind...

I had just finished my morning coffee break and was approaching the Highway 101 overpass. From the opposite direction, a car drove up to my marked sheriff's unit and flashed its lights at me, the driver's arm waving wildly through his open window. I pulled to a stop beside him and he breathlessly exclaimed that there had just been a terrible head-on collision on the highway. I drove to the top of the overpass and spotted what looked like smoke, dust and steam about a half-mile down the freeway. Racing to the scene, I radioed an "11-83" (traffic accident, no details yet), to dispatch and requested that the California Highway Patrol respond. As the adrenaline kicked in, I uttered my usual half-prayer, "God, I hate accidents."

The scene was carnage. A head-on collision had occurred between a large station wagon and a smaller sedan in the fast lane of the freeway. I saw a father and small son in the sedan.

7

The father had put his son in a car seat in front, turned the seat into the correct rear-facing position, but had not secured the car seat with the belt. The infant seat had rocketed forward on impact, crushing the dashboard of the car, and the boy was in shock with unknown injuries. The father was pinned behind the steering wheel, screaming in agony from his injuries. I discovered later that they both survived.

I rushed to the station wagon to determine the situation. When I came up to the passenger door and looked inside, I spotted two little, old ladies in their church dresses, both wedged face-up under the crushed dashboard. The driver did not move, except for a shocked, blinking stare. She died at the hospital. I heard a gurgling sound from the passenger and saw bloody bubbles on her dying lips. As I reached through the shattered window to remove a protruding denture from this sweet lady's mouth, she stopped her struggles and was gone...

"Are you going to call?" my wife held my cell phone with a questioning look on her face. I shook myself out of my former nightmare and re-engaged the present one. I tried dialing 9-1-1, but we were in a dead cellular zone. I had to wait a couple of minutes before I could get through to the Colorado Highway Patrol dispatcher. She said she would advise the Utah Highway Patrol because she had no units in position. After I hung up, my wife and I prayed the driver wouldn't kill anyone. I tried to forget both nightmares. My daughter never even woke up.

How in the world could these wrong-way drivers possibly manage to ignore all the obvious signs that they were on a deadly path to destruction? The little old lady in the earlier incident was probably confused by age. I have no clue about the more recent event. Was this driver also confused by age? Suicidal? Alcohol or drug-impaired? Grossly inattentive? Preoccupied? Lulled by habit into an unsafe "autopilot" attitude?

We can only imagine the drivers' thoughts if they believed they were on the right side of the road, "Who are all these crazy people coming at me in my lane, passing cars in such an unsafe manner? Who turned around all the signs? How come they painted a yellow stripe on the shoulder on my side of the road and a white stripe on the shoulder of the other lane? Did they run out of one kind of paint? How come all the road reflectors are turned the wrong way? Who put those pesky red signs at the freeway on-ramp to distract me from finding my radio station?"

Partner, here is the spiritual application to this story. As regular as clockwork, I speak with people who are driving the wrong way on the road of life. When I try to point out that fact on the basis of God's Word, they sometimes insist that the spiritual signs are all turned around, that others are going the wrong way, or that someone laid out life's lines wrong. Sometimes, their thinking is chemically impaired, or they are spiritually inattentive or maybe they are suicidal and just don't care anymore.

I know, based on God's Word and experience, that each of us is regularly tempted to drive the wrong way onto a spiritu-al off-ramp. Some of us are hell-bent southbound in the northbound fast lane of life. We may think we are right as rain the entire time, but, in fact, are placing ourselves and others (typically the ones we love the most) at terrible risk. This is why God always urges us to react *now* to the spiritual dangers we face—in our personal or professional lives, our marriages, our families, our friendships and anything else in our lives that is at risk. The Bible, God's road sign for life, calls us to repentance. "Repentance" literally means to have a change of mind by the power of the Holy Spirit. Repentance is a turning away from sin and a turning back to God. He calls us to stop on our wrong-way road, turn around and go the right way. And, remember, Jesus said, "I am the Way." (John 14:6). Because of the cross of Christ we have been set on the right road through the free gift of God's forgiveness and friendship.

Don't wind up as an accidental hood ornament on the Mack truck of life.

Don't wind up as an accidental hood ornament on the Mack truck of life. Take a look at your life NOW and see what lane you are in and what direction you are heading. Don't risk being a wrong-way driver.

Father in heaven,

Keep me from flying down the freeway of life the wrong way. Help me always read the road signs in your word, so that I don't make a wrong turn with my decisions and get lost on the spiritual streets. Keep me attentive to the dangerous traffic of this world and help me drive defensively around the devil. Help me follow your directions and rely on your transport, so that some day I will safely reach my destination in heaven with you,

Amen.

A TINY CORNER

A PEACE OFFICER FRIEND OF MINE ONCE OBSERVED, "We live in just a tiny corner of the universe. No matter how smart we are or how hard we try, we can never go much past that little corner of knowledge and experience. How can we be sure of anything? How can we have hope?"

My friend was exactly right. On our own, we are limited in our knowledge and beliefs. On our own, we cannot ultimately be sure of anything. The Creator of the universe must reveal himself to us if we are to know our place and purpose in the universe. He must speak to us if we are to hope. The Good News is that he has spoken. We are not lost in a corner. The loving God of the universe—Father, Son, and the Holy Spirit—speaks to us in his Word. He addresses our needs and gives us his life.

> "Your word is a lamp for my feet and a light for my path." *Psalm 119:105*

SPIRITUAL "SITUATIONAL AWARENESS"

SOME COPS THINK THAT BEING "RELIGIOUS" IS A crutch. You may be one of those cops. In fact, you may think that relying on God is a sign of weakness. However, this mindset is a denial of our actual situation and the actual solution. None of us is John Wayne. *Even John Wayne wasn't John Wayne.* The truth is, a person of faith happily exchanges the many ineffective crutches that tempt us for the true foundational strength that is found only in God's Word. An officer who recognizes this is exercising spiritual situational awareness—spiritual street smarts—and is more likely to survive in the ways that ultimately count.

It is interesting to note that scientific research also shows that faith makes a measurable, positive difference in our lives (e.g. "Faith is Powerful Medicine," *Reader's Digest*, October, 1999). Faith, and the God in whom that faith is placed, are real. God makes a difference in our lives—and that's no crutch, partner, that's reality!

As peace officers, we have a duty to protect and serve society, but we also have a prior duty to take care of ourselves so that we *can* protect and serve society! With this responsibility also comes an obligation to take care of those we love. Although there are many who can replace us in our professional duties, no one can replace us in our families. The untimely loss of a family member through death, divorce, or other tragedy is devastating. Although it is true that professional law enforcement requires sacrifice, it does not mean unnecessary and inappropriate sacrifice. Significantly, the better we address our personal and family needs, the better we

Each one of us needs to ask ourselves, "Am I spiritually and situationally aware?"

serve society. Do we ultimately serve society if we let ourselves and our families, "go to hell in a hand basket?" Don't some of society's biggest problems stem from neglect and abuse of self and family? Each one of us needs to ask ourselves, "Am I spiritually and situationally aware?"

> Lord,
> Sometimes I get tunnel vision and have trouble seeing the big picture; because I'm not you. I need your help. Help me look at life the way it really is and not just how I think it is. Help me take care of myself and those I love. Don't let me ever make the mistake of thinking that my trusting you is a sign of weakness, but instead help me always understand that only by trusting you will I be truly aware and strong,
> Amen.

"Blessed is the person who does not follow the advice of wicked people, take the path of sinner, or join the company of mockers. Rather, he delights in the teachings of the Lord and reflects on his teachings day and night. He is like a tree planted beside streams—a tree that produces fruit in season and whose leaves do not wither. He succeeds in everything he does. Wicked people are not like that. Instead, they are like husks that the wind blows away." *Psalm 1:1-4*

CAN A COP BE A
CHRISTIAN?

FLANKED BY TWO POLICE OFFICERS, I WALKED INTO
the Denver radio station. We were there as talk show
guests. The topic of the broadcast was law enforcement and
for an hour and a half, the three of us, all professing
Christians, fielded phone calls and questions. One of the talk
show hosts asked, "Can a cop be a Christian?"

For years, I have heard variations of this question from
people both inside and outside of law enforcement, from
Christians and non-Christians. Assumptions often prompt
this question. For example, some people think, "Cops carry
guns. If they use them, don't they break the commandment
that says, 'Thou shalt not kill?' Doesn't their willingness to use
deadly force preclude them from being Christians?"

Some who ask this question may be thinking about the
old King James version of the Ten Commandments, which
say, "Thou shalt not kill" (Exodus 20:13), or they may be
thinking about the statement Jesus made during his famous
sermon on the Mount (Matthew 5:21). They may think that
all killing is wrong and forbidden by God. Let's address this
incorrect view.

We must first remember that the Bible was not originally written in English. In the original Hebrew of Exodus 20:13, as well as in the original Greek of Matthew 5:21, the word "kill" is not used. The word, "murder" is used. Modern translations use, "murder" instead of "kill" in these passages, thus correcting this possible misunderstanding. God's Word allows killing in certain instances, such as defense of life, capital punishment and fighting a just war. Scripture makes a point of praising law enforcement. Romans 13:1-7 lays the foundation for the good and necessary role peace officers play in society. It defines both the authority and the mission of law enforcement.

> **Sometimes an officer feels he or she cannot be both a cop and a Christian because the requirements and realities of both seem so contradictory.**

Officers "bear the sword" for a good reason. When you wield that sword—that force—in a lawful way, you are acting as a minister or servant of God. Your use of proper force is not a necessary evil. It is a necessary good. We can boldly say on the basis of God's Word that all officers have a clear duty to use reasonable and necessary force, including deadly force, when justified. Sometimes an officer feels he or she cannot be both a cop and a Christian because the requirements and realities of both seem so contradictory. Officers are told to be tough. Christians are told the meek shall inherit the earth. Officers operate by the law. Christians operate by grace.

Officers uphold justice. Christians uphold mercy. Officers are prepared to use force, even deadly force, in the discharge of their duties. Christians are prepared to turn the other cheek. Officers look for suspicious circumstances and suspect people, or they wind up deceived or, worse yet, dead. Christians look for the good, the lovely, and the praiseworthy. Law enforcement requires negative reinforcement. Christianity requires positive reinforcement.

However, don't let appearances fool you. These contrasts are not the whole story. When we study the Bible, we find a Christian's world is not opposed to a cop's world, but instead includes that world in a broader reality. Conversely, to avoid becoming too narrow and negative, a cop's reality needs a Christian's reality.

Stay with me on this one. It's important. God deals with humans in two distinct ways—using his law and his love. Both ways are his ways. They may appear contradictory, but, in fact, they are complementary. For important professional *and* personal reasons, we need to clearly understand these two "jurisdictions" of law and love. If officers are misinformed about Christianity, they can easily become confused by these contrasting jurisdictions. This confusion can then drive officers away from a God some may perceive as too just and, ironically, others may perceive as too merciful.

Let's consider each of God's jurisdictions of law and love in turn. Because our imperfect world needs justice and order, God provides his law to guide society and restrain evil. His law also guides us in our personal moral lives. It also shows us our need for a Savior apart from obedience to the law, because none of us has kept God's law perfectly (God requires perfection according to his law, because he is perfect). You need not be a Christian to understand or accept God's law. God has revealed it to every human heart by nature (Romans 1:20, Romans 2:14-15). God has codified this natural law in the Ten Commandments. It is also found in the Golden Rule (Matthew 7:12, and also note that the Golden Rule finds expression in the writings of Jews, Moslems, Hindus, Buddhists, Confucianists, Taoists, and Zoroastrainists). Natural law has also been codified in society's laws. It is God's will that human affairs be governed by laws that are just and fair (Proverbs 29).

> **Justice demands that we are punished or rewarded according to our merits or our deeds.**

According to Romans 13, God endorses the enforcement of laws by both the civil and military authority. He also endorses punishment, including capital punishment, for violators of the law ("an eye for an eye," the principle of proportional punishment, is prescribed in Exodus 21:24). God's law should always govern the State and its citizens.

Law focuses on what we do. It is performance oriented. Law also requires justice. Justice demands that we are punished or rewarded according to our merits or our deeds. The law knows nothing of forgiveness. A simple sense of right and wrong, or fear or reward, motivates those who live under the law. We must live primarily by the law in our professional lives and should also apply the law's guidance in our personal lives.

Now, let's address God's jurisdiction of love. God's Word says that God is love (1 John 4:16). God's love is primarily expressed in the gift of his Son Jesus Christ, who died to atone for the sins of the whole world. The law of God, because it demands perfect performance and justice, would condemn us all to hell were it not for the intervention of Christ, who in love as the perfect Son of God took our punishment on himself. This good news of God's love — the Gospel — is revealed by God not in our hearts by nature, but through his Son (John 1:1-18, Hebrews 1:1-3). The Gospel is

> **The only requirement to receive love's reward of forgiveness and eternal life is to simply receive this heavenly gift in faith by the power of the Holy Spirit.**

also revealed in the pages of Scripture, where we find the good news of God's Son (Romans 10:5-17, 2 Peter 1:20-21).

The message of God's love contained in the Gospel, unlike God's law, focuses on what Jesus Christ has done, not on what we do. His love is unconditional. It is given to everyone, apart from merits or deeds. The only requirement to receive love's reward of forgiveness and eternal life is to simply receive this heavenly gift in faith by the power of the Holy Spirit. As Christians, we are to extend this unconditional love to all our personal relationships ("...turn the other cheek," Jesus' imperative for love, is found in his Sermon on the Mount in Matthew 5:38-39). This love knows nothing about punishment. It is motivated solely by God's love in Christ.

Obviously, God's two jurisdictions are as opposite as night and day, and yet the same God rules both. How do we explain this apparent paradox? How do we live according to both jurisdictions without going nuts? Many officers believe it is not possible or prudent to do so, and, unfortunately, give up on the idea of being a Christian.

We must first understand that God did not originally intend it to be this way. God created us to live in a perfect world under one undivided jurisdiction of love and holiness. But when we fell into sin and the world was no longer a perfect place, God was faced with a seemingly impossible dilemma. Love and holiness become contradictory concepts when applied to sinful human beings. How could God maintain both his perfect love, which requires mercy and forgiveness for us sinners, and at the same time maintain his perfect holiness, which requires justice and punishment for us sinners?

> **I once heard a radio preacher say that he did not think he had committed any sins during the previous three days. My first thought was "Let's talk to your wife."**

God's answer was to send his holy and loving Son Jesus Christ, who demonstrated God's perfect mercy and justice by taking our punishment upon himself on the cross. In this way, he was able to be both loving *and* just. Psalm 85:10 says, "Mercy and truth have met. Righteousness and peace have kissed." In commenting on this, the famous sixteenth century church reformer and theologian Martin Luther noted that

God's holiness and love kiss at the cross of Jesus Christ. The dilemma is solved. The cross of Christ is God's perfect solution to provide what we need (forgiveness and eternal life), and preserve who he is (perfect love and righteousness).

We still have a problem, however. Although we have the free gift of forgiveness of sins and eternal life because of Christ, we are still imperfect people, whether or not we are Christians (I once heard a radio preacher say that he did not think he had committed any sins during the previous three days. My first thought was "Let's talk to your wife. She can probably enlighten us both." My second thought was that his claim was actually an unintended admission that he suffered from the sins of spiritual blindness and pride).

Although God has given us the eternal solution to our dilemma, in this imperfect world he, and we, must still operate according to his separate jurisdictions. The one jurisdiction is ruled by his perfect righteousness according to law and justice. The other is ruled by his perfect love according to mercy and forgiveness. It is important to understand that both jurisdictions are good and necessary, because God is the author and ruler of both. Any problems we have with this truth are a result of our own blindness and sin.

We need to understand and correctly apply God's two jurisdictions of law and love. Because we must have order and fairness in the world, we need to apply the law to society. We must also apply it to our personal moral conduct. But, in order to have hope, because the law points out our sin and the fact that we are less than perfect, we need to apply God's love to our personal lives, and extend that love to our personal relationships.

An officer cannot forgive and forget a felony action. The perpetrator must be arrested. A Christian officer, like any other officer, must apply the law in a lawful and just manner, including the legal and just use of force. This is entirely consistent with God's word. At the same time, he or she needs to demonstrate an attitude of God's love, especially in personal relationships. This, too, is entirely consistent with God's word. Above all, officers must rely on faith for spiritual strength in every circumstance. Maintaining a proper balance between law and love will ensure an officer's professional and personal well-being.

> **Justice, tempered with mercy, should be our modus operandi professionally. Mercy, tempered with justice, should be our modus operandi personally.**

An officer needs to correctly apply God's two jurisdictions. Because officers spend so much time with the law in their professional existence, they especially need the counterbalance of God's love in their personal lives. Some officers, even some Christian officers, do not understand this and incorrectly apply the law harshly to every aspect of life. This legalistic mindset creates a huge amount of stress and is one reason why officers can be at such high risk physically, emotionally, relationally, and spiritually. On the one hand, the law of God, improperly applied, can make a basket case of our personal lives. On the other hand, the love of God, improperly applied, can make a basket case of our professional lives. Justice, tempered with mercy, should be our modus operandi professionally. Mercy, tempered with justice, should be our modus operandi personally. All beliefs, actions and attitudes should be motivated by self-sacrificing love.

God's two jurisdictions can be difficult to grasp, but when you understand and apply these truths, you will be a good cop *and* a good Christian. Officers should be encouraged, not discouraged, by God's Word. There is compatibility, not conflict, in a cop being a Christian. Rather than being a roadblock, Christianity paves the way to a clear understanding of the good and God-pleasing role of peace officers. The question is not, "Can a cop be a Christian," but rather, "How can a cop *not* be a Christian?"

Father in heaven,

Thank you for showing me that being a Christian is not a hindrance, but instead a help to being a cop. Thank you that I can have pride in my role, since that role comes straight from you. Help me to be faithful in my role as an officer and faithful in my identity as a Christian. May these never come in conflict due to weakness on my part, but help me live with integrity always,

Amen.

YOUR AUTHORITY AS A
PEACE OFFICER

L AW ENFORCEMENT IS NOT A "NECESSARY EVIL." IT IS
a divinely ordained "good." A peace officer's authority
comes from God. Officers have a God-given duty to use lawful and necessary force in the discharge of those duties. We
all have a responsibility to honor and submit to lawful authority and to support those who govern us.

"Every person should obey the government in
power. No government would exist if it hadn't been
established by God. The governments which exist have
been put in place by God. Therefore, whoever resists the
government opposes what God has established. Those
who resist will bring punishment on themselves.

People who do what is right don't have to be afraid of
the government. But people who do what is wrong should
be afraid of it. Would you like to live without being afraid
of the government? Do what is right, and it will praise you.
The government is God's servant working for your good.

But if you do what is wrong, you should be afraid. The government has the right to carry out the death sentence. It is God's servant, an avenger to execute God's anger on anyone who does what is wrong. Therefore, it is necessary for you to obey, not only because you're afraid of God's anger but also because of your own conscience.

That is also why you pay your taxes. People in the government are God's servants while they do the work he has given them. Pay everyone whatever you owe them. If you owe taxes, pay them. If you owe tolls, pay them. If you owe someone respect, respect that person. If you owe someone honor, honor that person." *Romans 13:1-7*

OUR BACKUP

Life is full of surprises, good and bad.
Life is full of things that are outside of our control.
Life is full of times when we feel alone and need someone
     who understands and cares.
Life is full of times when we don't know what to think or
     what to do.
Life is full of success and joy, as well as failure and sorrow.
Life is full of many things that are simply beyond us...
In this full life that we live, we have a friend who walks with
     us, a friend who is beyond those things that are beyond us:
He is there when others are not.
He supports us when others do not.
He loves us when others will not.
He gives us backup when others cannot.

Dear God,

Thank you that I can talk to you anytime, anywhere, and you hear me, even when I don't know what to say or how to say it. Thank you that I can be honest with you, whether I'm stressed or depressed, because you know me anyway, and love me no matter what. I'm sorry for those times when I have turned my back on you and refused your

forgiveness and help. Help me understand the truth that you are here to help and heal me. Thanks for giving me your Son, Jesus, who is the Friend who sticks closer than family. Thanks for giving me your Spirit, who helps me pray. Help me remember to come to you first, last, and always in every situation I face in life.

Thank you...

"...a loving friend can stick closer than family."
Proverbs 18:24

"At the same time the Spirit also helps us in our weakness, because we don't know how to pray for what we need. But the Spirit intercedes along with our groans that cannot be expressed in words." *Romans 8:26*

"...never stop praying."
1 Thessalonians 5:17

"We need to hold on to our declaration of faith: We have a superior chief priest who has gone through the heavens. That person is Jesus, the Son of God. We have a chief priest who is able to sympathize with our weaknesses. He was tempted in every way that we are, but he didn't sin. So we can go confidently to the throne of God's kindness to receive mercy and find kindness, which will help us at the right time." *Hebrews 4:14-16*

PROFILES IN COURAGE

I WITNESSED A GUTSY MOVE THAT NIGHT. I WAS WORKING out of the Sheriff's sub-station. Rob was one of my deputies. We were dispatched to a "man with a gun" call. The subject was reported to be intoxicated, belligerent and armed with a 30.06 rifle. So, being cautious—and a sergeant—I graciously allowed Rob to take point with his patrol car. I followed in my marked 4 X 4 unit. As we approached the rural scene, I killed my headlights to avoid back-lighting Rob to the advantage of our drunk friend. Instead, I used my spotlight to sweep the area perimeter. Suddenly, in quick succession, I saw three things happen.

First, a young boy appeared on the side of the road. Next, from behind some bushes, a man slowly rose out of the darkness from a crouched position. He was about fifteen to twenty feet from Rob's car, with what looked to be a rifle in his hands. Then Rob hit his brakes and jumped out of the car. I jumped out of my vehicle also and started to pull my gun. But, surprisingly, instead of pulling his gun, Rob charged the suspect.

The race was on. The suspect wobbled to his feet, raising his rifle in the general direction of Rob, the boy and myself. But, before the muzzle came level, Rob hit the man with a tackle that would have done a middle linebacker proud. I ran up to help, but the only thing left to do was stick a fork in the bad guy, because he was done. Good thing, too, because his 30.06 was loaded and ready to rock.

After the dust settled, Rob told me he could see that the guy was drunk and figured he could tackle and disarm him before he could react. He said he didn't want to get in a shootout because of the danger to the boy (cautious sergeants are expendable). Knowing Rob, I also figured he didn't want to shoot the suspect if he felt he had an option, even if it was a risky one. So, he made an instant decision and rolled the dice. He made a gutsy move because he left cover with his gun holstered. He made the right call because it worked. He was razor close between being "dumb-stupid" and "smart-brave." Smart-brave won. Rob received a letter of commendation from his sergeant. The sheriff concurred.

> **If courage dies, people die. If courage lives, people live. "To protect and serve" demands courage.**

"To protect and serve" is the foundational motivation and mission for all good law enforcement officers. Along with proper training, equipment and teamwork, officers must have well-honed character to properly answer their high calling. Along with integrity, honesty, dedication, self-sacrifice and other virtues, officers must possess courage. Courage is the indispensable engine that drives all those other virtues, as well as all that training, equipment and teamwork, into harm's way, out on the street, where an officer must go to get the job done.

If courage dies, people die. If courage lives, people live. "To protect and serve" demands courage. Rob demonstrated courage that dark night and so proved he was a good cop.

Former President John F. Kennedy once wrote a book titled *Profiles in Courage*. In it, he detailed fascinating accounts of ordinary people who stepped up in difficult situations to earn that special badge called, "courage." But, we can't really talk about courage without considering the ultimate profile in courage.

First, let's pause for a moment to ask, "What is the main message of Christianity?" What does it mean to you? If you like, write out your answer. I've posed this challenge many times. The responses have varied from, "Obey the Ten Commandments," "Do unto others as they do unto you," (The Golden Rule) "Love God and others," and "Be filled with God's Spirit," to "Be the best I can be." Many of the answers I hear are directly related to what we "should" do or be. Let me say

> **The main message of the Christian faith is not about what we should do or be, but about who Jesus Christ is and what he has done for us.**

that, although these answers are all part of Christianity, they are not the main message. The main message of the Christian faith is not about what we should do or be.

Let me give you a clue to God's answer to this question by asking, "What is probably the most well-known verse in the entire Bible?" For those of you who are bigger football fans than Bible fans, the clue is found in the poster so prominently displayed by that fan at nationally televised football games. You've probably guessed it by now—John 3:16. This verse says, "God loved the world this way—He gave His only Son so that everyone who believes in Him will not die but will have eternal life."

The main message of the Christian faith is not about what we should do or be, but about who Jesus Christ is and what he has done for us. He is the one who has acted on our behalf. We only need to trust him. This is an absolutely critical distinction to understand. Of all people, officers should understand the importance of this point. Each day, officers are confronted with the sad fact that humankind is not capable of keeping the Ten Commandments, that people do not live by the Golden Rule, that even people with the best intentions sometimes fail to love God and others and that, too often, we push away the Spirit of God instead of filling our lives with His Spirit. More than most people, officers understand that the best we can do or be is not nearly good enough—especially when judged by God's standard of perfection. Spiritually, on our own, we are in an "officer down" condition. Apart from Jesus Christ, we are spiritually dead and incapable of earning God's favor.

So, let's go back to the ultimate profile in courage. I often ask officers to name the top ten qualities of a good cop. Then I ask, "Who is the worst criminal in history?" And, finally, "Who saved the most people from this ultimate bad guy in the biggest hostage rescue of all time?" The answers are obvious. Jesus Christ possesses every good quality you can name in a cop. He confronted the worst perpetrator in all of history, Satan himself, and took him down. He had to act to save us—

and here we come to the profile in courage. Because of his courage, Jesus Christ freed us from the clutches of Satan and brought hope and life to the entire world. The foundational motivation and the mission of Jesus Christ is to protect and to serve all humankind. Isn't that an amazing profile in courage?

The Bible says, "… he emptied himself by taking on the form of a servant, by becoming like other humans, by having a human appearance. He humbled himself by becoming obedient to the point of death, death on a cross. This is why God has given him an exceptional honor—the name honored above all other names—so that at the name of Jesus everyone in heaven, on earth, and in the world below will kneel and confess that Jesus Christ is Lord to the glory of God the Father." Philippians 2:7-11

The main message of Christianity is about love. Not ours—his. His love prompted the greatest act of courage in all of history, performed by the greatest peace officer who ever walked in harm's way. His was the courage of the cross. Remember that, not just at Christmas and Easter, but always.

Jesus,

Help me be smart-brave and not dumb-stupid in life. Give me your courage in every situation to be the right person and do the right thing. Help me also live the truth that to protect and serve others, I need you to protect and serve me. Remind me always that faith first and foremost trusts what you freely do for me, not what I am obliged to do for you, so that I can have peace in you and courage to face the foe, no matter what—win, lose, or draw.

Amen.

"Look at it this way: At the right time, while we were still helpless, Christ died for ungodly people. Finding someone who would die for a godly person is rare. Maybe someone would have the courage to die for a good person. Christ died for us while we were still sinners. This demonstrates God's love for us. Since Christ's blood has now given us God's approval, we are even more certain that Christ will save us from God's anger. If the death of his Son restored our relationship with God while we were still his enemies, we are even more certain that, because of this restored relationship, the life his Son lived will save us. In addition, our Lord Jesus Christ lets us continue to brag about God. After all, it is through Christ that we now have this restored relationship with God."
Romans 5:6-11

JESUS CHRIST, THE
ULTIMATE PEACE OFFICER

"**A** CHILD WILL BE BORN FOR US. A SON WILL BE GIVEN to us. The government will rest on his shoulders. He will be named: Wonderful Counselor, Mighty God, Everlasting Father, Prince of Peace." Isaiah 9:6

MY UNSEEN PARTNER

T HE ELDERLY LADY WITH THE SMILING YOUNG EYES approached me after church and took my hand in both of hers. "You're 203," she boldly announced. "203" was, in fact, my radio call sign as a patrol sergeant. Surprised by this comment from a total stranger, I asked her, "How did you know that?" Her eyes twinkled. "I heard you were coming to our church to visit today. I have a radio scanner at home and I always listen to you boys." I smiled back at her. "I hope you pray as well as listen—we need all the help we can get!" She didn't miss a beat. "Oh, I do! I do!" she eagerly responded, and then introduced herself. "My name's Lucille and I really enjoy following all of you as you take calls." I discovered that, because I had gone off-duty at 2 a.m. that morning and had discussed my appearance at church, Lucille

> **I discovered during this enjoyable conversation that, although I never knew it, I had an "unseen partner" in Lucille.**

had eavesdropped on my radio traffic conversation to get the details. As she enthusiastically continued, I realized one of the

main occupations in the life of this dear Christian lady was listening to and praying for her "boys." "I know all the boys' call
numbers and I've learned all your radio codes," Lucille said
proudly. I discovered during this enjoyable conversation that,
although I never knew it, I had an "unseen partner" in Lucille.
She had apparently been praying for me and all the officers for
some time.

On duty later that day, I met Tim, one of my resident
deputies, on an isolated stretch of seacoast highway. After
briefing and an exchange of
paperwork, we drove off toward
our respective beats. I was just
settling in for the long drive
back, when my radio jarred me
upright. "11-99! 11-99!" I
couldn't believe it. Tim was des-
perately calling for help. My
heart jumped as I quickly
scanned the road for a turn-
around. "No warning at all," I thought to myself. "How could
he get into so much trouble so fast?" I wondered, as I raced
back to find him. On the way, I listened to Tim broadcast a
description of a firewood-laden truck that had struck his
patrol car head-on and then limped away—in my direction.

The thought came to me, "No more backup. Not enough backup."

A minute later, I found the damaged truck pulled off to the
side of the road, with its inebriated and belligerent driver next
to it. I quickly wrestled the man into my unit and then continued on to assist Tim. The accident scene was a mess. Tim was
bleeding from the head and was obviously going into shock,
but he was stoically trying to direct traffic around his demol-

ished car and firewood and broken glass strewn everywhere. I carefully guided him into my vehicle and then worked to stabilize the scene.

As I moved from first aid for Tim in the front seat, to a drunk and violent prisoner in the back seat, and traffic control on the highway, the radio interrupted my "Triage Dance of the Sheriff's Sergeant." My one remaining deputy was being dispatched to an in-progress shooting many miles away. I grabbed my radio mike to have dispatch get backup, "Off-duty deputy, reserve, highway patrol officer, fish and game warden, state park ranger, somebody, anybody." The thought came to me, "No more backup. Not enough backup."

To my intense relief, dispatch located another deputy for the shooting call and he and the primary officer raced to the scene together. A short time later, however, my worst fears were realized when I heard a frantic radio call, "Shots fired!" My deputies were being shot at, and I could do nothing about it. I kicked at a piece of firewood in frustration and anger.

It was not until later, after the accident was cleaned up, after Tim was released from the hospital, after both the drunk driver and the shooter (who missed my deputies) were booked at the jail, after all the noise had quieted and all the dust had settled, that I had time to remember Lucille. You see, we did have backup. We had Lucille. Lucille had been listening. Lucille had been praying.

I learned a lot from Lucille. She taught me that she cared and was praying for me, and that others also cared and were praying for law enforcement officers. She reminded me that, in a lonely and dangerous job, I wasn't alone. Despite the demoralizing opposition officers often encounter, there are a lot of people who support and pray for them—people we may never see this side of heaven.

Most of all, Lucille reminded me of another unseen Friend who cares—the One who is our Ultimate Backup Partner. He is there for us even when we do not realize it—even if we have not yet come to call on him. He is our protector. He proved it by taking the bullet that was meant for us, by dying on the cross in our place, and by giving us the free gift of forgiveness and eternal life. Jesus Christ is the ultimate backup for the "officer needs help" situations of my life—and yours.

Have you called on Him?

Lord,

Sometimes the constant conflict I face forces me into tunnel vision—and I see only death and destruction and despair. Help me remember when I am rolling around in the mud and the blood and the beer that there really are people out there who do care and are praying for me, and that you care, too. Remind me that your own word says that my calling is as sacred to you as the preacher's, that I am a minister of your divine law, and that a lot of folks know that and support me in my mission. Remind me that the only reason I don't get to meet them more often is that I generally don't get called to their homes in the middle of the night to break up a domestic—but they are really there and they really care. Back them up, too, Lord, because it's a jungle out there sometimes.

Thanks again...

"First of all, I encourage you to make petitions, prayers, intercessions, and prayers of thanks for all people, for rulers, and for everyone who has authority over us. Pray for these people so that we can have a quiet and peaceful life always lived in a godly and reverent way. This is good and pleases God our Savior. He wants all people to be saved and to learn the truth. There is one God. There is also one mediator between God and humans—a human, Christ Jesus. He sacrificed himself for all people to free them from their sins." *I Timothy 2:1-6*

THE BARBED WIRE

THERE IS A VITAL RELATIONSHIP BETWEEN GOOD LAW enforcement and the Good Lawgiver.

Law enforcement must be built upon authority.

Authority must be built upon law.

Law must be built upon justice.

Justice must be built upon principles.

Principles must be built upon truth.

Truth must be universal.

Universal truth must be authored by a universal Creator.

Professional law enforcement requires peace officers to stand firm on principle. Principles provide the solid foundation on which stable protection and service to society are built.

In remarking on one very basic principle, an officer described the thin blue line by saying, "We are the barbed wire that separates the sheep from the wolves." The role of officers is to stand between violators and victims. That role comes from God and from the state (statutory law). Officers defend society with that force which is reasonable and necessary, including deadly force, if need be. In this tough duty, an officer needs God's tempering truth, from which the steel of strong law and life are formed. To live otherwise is to also become a violator or a victim. Principle, based upon God-given precepts, gives the wire its strength.

We cannot govern principle. Principle must govern us—not power, or party or person. Lack of principle is what begets the wolf of dictatorship in a people or degeneracy in a person. If we deny God and his universal truth, we usurp him and author our own truth and invent our own self-centered pseudo-principles. We then turn into wolves ourselves, destroying one another in a Darwinian fight to the death…and justice goes the way of the unprotected sheep.

> **There is a vital relationship between good law enforcement and the Good Lawgiver.**

Spirit of God,

Give me your power so I can be strong to stand between the sheep and the wolves; so that I will never be a victim or a perpetrator, but always and only, a servant and protector. In my work, govern me by your principles of law and justice, seasoned by the compassion and mercy you show me. I pray in Jesus' name,

Amen.

"O Lord, your word is established in heaven forever. Your faithfulness endures throughout every generation. You set the earth in place, and it continues to stand. All things continue to stand today because of your regulations, since they are all your servants. If your teachings had not made me happy, then I would have died in my misery. I will never forget your guiding principles, because you gave me a new life through them. I am yours. Save me, because I have searched for your guiding principles. The wicked people have waited for me in order to destroy me, yet, I want to understand your written instructions. I have seen a limit to everything else, but your commandments have no limit. *Psalm 119:89-96*

A QUESTION OF INTEGRITY

YEARS AGO, SOME RADICAL MEMBERS OF A DOMESTIC terrorist group were cornered by officers on the West Coast. An epic firefight followed, during which the officers remodeled the suspects' house with thousands of rounds of ammunition. The story goes that, while these officers were unselfishly administering these megadoses of lead poisoning, some motor officers working the outer perimeter got bored handling looky-loo traffic and decided to join in the fun. They apparently alternated between directing traffic and cranking off revolver shots in the general direction of the bad guys, *over the heads of their inner perimeter partners*, thus meeting everyone's daily requirement of adrenaline and giving new meaning to the word, "redundant."

As I look back at the past, I also remember a president under siege. The chief law enforcement officer of the United States was publicly impeached at the end of what began as private behavior. While it might satisfy some daily adrenaline requirement to lob some more political projectiles in the direction of William Jefferson Clinton, it would serve no appropriate purpose here, and would certainly be redundant. What *does* concern me—leaving politics aside—is that the Clinton Capers should give each of us a personal reason to pause and reflect on our rights and responsibilities as public and private persons and to consider the consequences of our beliefs and behavior. No matter what our political persuasion, the president's impeachment cracks open the door to that hidden room called "the human condition," to reveal a full-sized mirror within. Individually, we all need to look in that mirror to see if we stand impeached before God.

"What do you think is the most important character quality of a good law enforcement officer?" I have asked this question of officers across the country and their answer is almost always the same: Integrity. Let's take a look at that word and what it should mean for us. What is integrity? Webster's Dictionary defines integrity as, "an unimpaired condition ... soundness...firm adherence to a code of esp. moral or artistic values ... incorruptibility ... the quality or state of being complete or undivided... syn{onym} see honesty ... ant{onym} see duplicity..."

> **Law enforcement forms a thin blue line to publicly protect us from a multitude of predators.**

Why do officers need integrity? Law enforcement forms a thin blue line to publicly protect us from a multitude of predators. Officers need significant tools to face this significant threat. Society hands officers these tools by vesting them with more discretionary authority and immediate power (including deadly force) than any other civil profession. In their exercise, these tools require the highest possible standards of personal conduct to avoid misuse. Without integrity, corruption and abuse of power *will* result and officers *will* become the perpetrators of those very things against which they are supposed to protect.

Without integrity, officers become predators themselves. You and I can both think of sad examples of this truth

Inherent in the word "integrity" is the idea of a strong and noble unity, a consistency of good qualities that adorns our being and purpose. Corruption, abuse, trickery—these are all excluded. Integrity is not a weather vane of convenience that shifts in the slightest breeze of opportunity, but rather a rock of conviction that remains unmovable in the storm of opposition. Integrity's compass is neither pain nor pleasure, but always what is right, and good, and best—apart from personal considerations. Integrity requires consistency of belief, word, attitude and action, both in public and in private. Integrity knows that duty is neither public nor private, but, instead, personal, principled and all-pervasive. Integrity demands courage just as it provides courage, honor, honesty and selflessness. Integrity never considers rights apart from responsibilities. Integrity, because it incorporates and unites all good characteristics, wraps every virtue in its arms. Thus, integrity is the greatest of all moral qualities.

> **Integrity, because it incorporates and unites all good characteristics, wraps every virtue in its arms.**

Enter the villain: To know is not necessarily to do. Each of us has had, and will periodically have, a breakdown of integrity in our lives. Integrity is a perfect ideal and we are all imperfect people. Even the Apostle Paul personally struggled with this unhappy truth (Romans 7:7-25). That being true, what are we to do? Let's look at the options.

Porn publisher Larry Flynt temporarily made a career out of defending Bill Clinton by "outing" politicians who had lapses of integrity. This lobbyist for moral midgetry basically suggested that we are all bottom-feeders and, therefore, anyone who aspires to rise above the muck is only trying to fool themselves and others. Larry's logic says, "To try is to fail. To fail is to become a hypocrite. To become a hypocrite is to actually commit the greatest crime against integrity. Therefore, why try? The only problem with a lack of moral integrity is the stigma attached by discreditable hypocrites. Get rid of the phony stigma and—presto!—no problem." However, there is a problem. Larry Flynt's inverted integrity is an integrity of the lowest common denominator—the sewer. How many of us want to live with our children down in that dark stench?

An apparently less extreme, but potentially just as dangerous, variation of the Larry Flynt theme is the idea of fitting in with the surrounding culture. This "integrity by poll" is popular with far too many people today. They do not ask whether something is fundamentally right or wrong, but only if it's "okay" with the culture. Their moral compass does not point to the true north of God-given principle, but is pulled from point to point by the fluctuating attraction of popular opinion. The problem with such a compass, however, is that we lose our way and go adrift. If our integrity only rises to the level of the culture, we will get trapped by that tide. What if a culture collectively flushes itself down the toilet, as Hitler's Germany did in the 1930's? Don't think it can't happen here. Popular culture today strives to pull us under on these currents of collective anti-integrity, which Winston Churchill once referred to as, "occult forces." Social and spiritual survival require a counteracting force of principled and courageous people, often acting with integrity above the level and against the drift of the surrounding culture. It is indeed true that the only thing necessary for evil to triumph is for good folks to do nothing.

Another option is to separate public and private integrity. Former President Clinton appealed to this distinction. This argument is a great temptation, especially for anyone who holds a public trust—including peace officers. The rationale runs something like this, "I work hard and sacrifice much on behalf of my public duties. I have a right to let the cork out a little in my private life, because it doesn't affect the public performance of my duties, doesn't hurt anyone but me, and it's nobody's business but my own." However, how often does private compromise lead to public shame and harm for ourselves and others? I can think of many

> **Here is a truth you can take to the bank: public integrity is a product of private integrity.**

examples of people who made this choice. You can, too. Apart from political considerations, how would Bill Clinton's family and fellow Americans answer the above question? How many of us have experienced the sad public consequences of our private transgressions, or are flirting with this disaster right now? Another problem is that private behavior often does involve at least one other person. That person gets burned and so do we, even if the behavior is "only private." Finally, and most importantly, right is right and wrong is wrong, whether or not an act is public or private (see God's take on secret sins in 2 Samuel 12:9-12).

Here is a truth you can take to the bank: public integrity is a product of private integrity. When private integrity goes down, public integrity will sink with it. Let me give an illustration. Many of the passengers of the Titanic never knew at the time that the great ship had hit an iceberg. At the time, many of the crew never suspected the seriousness of the breach, because it appeared to be so small compared to the size of the ship. Most of the Titanic, and all of the ship's surface above sea level, appeared to be in perfect shape. Ninety-nine percent of the ship was untouched by the collision, yet the damaged one percent was enough to sink the ship. The mighty Titanic lost its watertight integrity and the ocean took care of the rest. So it is with our own integrity. We may appear to all the world to be perfectly intact, and yet, below the calm surface of our public presence, we can receive a private mortal blow to our integrity. Our entire ship of life can be dragged down before God and everybody else into the depths.

Another option is to hide our compromised integrity behind a hypocritical façade of denial and self-righteousness. This is the temptation of the dishonest "religious person," as seen in Matthew 23. The problem here is that, even if we succeed in hiding our sin before the world, we lose all self-respect and still stand judged before God. Here we need to give the devil his rotted due. At our best, our motives are mixed and our sanctity is stained. It does not necessarily follow, however, that we should hide, make excuses or surrender integrity. Rather, honesty preserves integrity. We admit our fallibilities and call them what they are—sins. We repent, take our lumps if we have them coming, and move on. These are the attitudes and actions of a person of integrity who happens to be, just like everyone else, imperfect. Here it is important to point out that we can and should avoid gross sin in our lives, no matter what our spiritual orientation. Human frailty and fallibility are no excuse for "over the top" actions. Christian and non-Christian alike have a duty, an expectation, and an ability to avoid the worst forms of outward behavior. This knowledge of right and wrong is placed in every human heart, is known intuitively, and agrees with God's natural law (Romans 2:14-15).

God forgives. We must also forgive ourselves and others, get up, and go on.

Is there an alternative to Larry Flynt's inverted and drifting integrity, Bill Clinton's public/private parsing, or the Pharisee's religious hypocrisy? I suggest we affirm some age-old truths here. First, the world needs more, not less, integrity. Each of us should constantly strive for integrity in every area of our lives, great or small, public or private, no matter how difficult or how often we stumble (see Job 2:9-10 and Psalm 25, especially verse 21). Second, just because we stumble and fall does not mean we must remain in the mud. God forgives. We must also forgive ourselves and others, get up, and go on (Matthew 18:21-25, Luke 11:4, John 8:1-11).

Third, there are just and proper consequences to lapses of integrity, even if our human condition makes those lapses unavoidable. These consequences may take a variety of forms. They act to inhibit and restrain our bad behavior and also act as a future deterrent. They make us think twice. It's like I used to tell my drunk clients who didn't want to go along with the program, "You can go the easy way, or you can go the hard way—but you're gonna go." There needs to be consequences for breakdowns of integrity. For example, King David himself, although repentant and forgiven by God, still had to face terrible, but just, consequences for his sin.

> **The chain of character is only as strong as its weakest link. Integrity forges and tempers the whole.**

Fourth, to find true healing and happiness in our lives, we must always be careful to be honest before God and repent of our lapses of integrity. Jesus himself teaches us to do this in the Lord's prayer (Luke 11:4) and elsewhere (e.g. Luke 18:9-14). It is amazing what God will do in our lives if we, in honesty and humility, let him. The Apostle John writes,

"This is the message we heard from Christ and are reporting to you: God is light, and there isn't any darkness in him. If we say, 'We have a relationship with God' and yet live in the dark, we're lying. We aren't being truthful. But if we live in the light in the same way that God is in the light, we have a relationship with each other. And the blood of his Son Jesus cleanses us from every sin. If we say, 'We aren't sinful' we are deceiving ourselves, and the truth is not in us. God is faithful and reliable. If we confess our sins, he forgives them and cleanses us from everything we've done wrong. If we say, 'We have never sinned,' we turn God into a liar and his Word is not in us." *1 John 1:5-10*

John here points out that God has harnessed his team of four horses to pull us through the lapses in our lives:

1. Self examination. Honestly confront your condition.

2. Confession. Admit lapses of integrity and agree with God.

3. Repentance. Experience a change of heart and life by the power of God's Spirit.

4. Forgiveness. Our free gift of God's grace; received by trusting Christ.

The chain of character is only as strong as its weakest link. Integrity forges and tempers the whole. Right now, whatever your spiritual condition (remember that God takes us just as we are), I invite you to join me in self-examination, and in this prayer of confession:

Father in heaven,
You are an amazing and holy God, but you know, and I find, that I am much less than amazing and much less than holy. I have sinned against you and others and violated what I know to be right. I admit to you that my integrity has lapsed in the following ways...(here I confess to him personally, specifically, without excuses and with remorse, my violations of his good law). Because of the integrity of Jesus Christ and what he has done for me on the cross, forgive me freely, according to your wonderful promises. Help me, by the mighty power of your Holy Spirit, to live a new life of integrity every day. In Jesus' name I pray, Amen.

IF GOD IS A LOVING GOD...

"**I**F GOD IS LOVING *AND* ALL-POWERFUL, WHY DOES he allow the evil and tragedy I see?" One of the toughest questions an officer confronts is this hard-hitting heavyweight, which can put an officer down in a heartbeat if he or she has no armor of God (Ephesians 6:10-18), and no spiritual backup (Psalm 50:15). Over the years, officers have routinely and reasonably nailed me with this sane question about a sometimes-insane world. You owe it to yourself to carefully study and pray through this issue with the help of God's word before you hit the mean streets, or you will wind up a bug on Satan's bumper.

> "If God is loving and all-powerful, why does he allow the evil and tragedy I see?"

As a peace officer, you work with the devil's dregs and senseless sorrow every day. You are especially sensitive to this question of evil and tragedy because of your experience. Sadly, a lack of understanding about that experience has driven some officers away from a God they perceive as either uncaring or impotent, and into a life of cynicism and despair. This is the hopeless answer of Job's wife, who advised him in his terrible tragedy, "Are you still holding on to your principles? Curse God and die!" (Job 2:9). However, as Job himself recognized, even in the horror of his loss (Job 2:10), this is no answer at all. Yes, we must seriously tackle this issue, but we must also trust that God, because he loves us, gives the answer we need.

To address this question properly, we should first turn to the account God gives us in Genesis that tells the story of the creation of humans in the Garden of Eden (Genesis 1-3). Adam and Eve, created as perfect human beings in the image of God, also individually received a free will—the capacity to choose good or evil (Genesis 1:27; Genesis 2:15-17). If they had not been created with this free will, they would not have been human. They would have been mere machines - mere robots. Furthermore, if there were no consequences following their choices, their free will would mean nothing. They would have been denied the dignity of human responsibility that provides meaning to our creation. For instance, if we make a bad choice and step in front of a moving freight train and nothing bad happens, it means nothing to choose *not* to step in front of the train, and so the decision either way is meaning-

> **The ability to choose good means nothing apart from the ability to also choose evil, with all the real consequences inherent in those true choices.**

less. By definition, there would be no good or bad choices because there would be no good or bad consequences. All of our choices, and therefore all of our existence, would become a farce. The ability to choose good means nothing apart from the ability to also choose evil, with all the real consequences inherent in those true choices. All would be pointless. This, in fact, was King Solomon's conclusion about "life under the sun" apart from God and his divinely ordered proper consequences (Ecclesiastes 1:14; 12:1-14). Here let me say that pointlessness might be better than pain if God did not provide us with his answer, but in Jesus Christ, our backup "Prince of Peace" officer, he does (Isaiah 9:6).

Adam and Eve fell for Satan's con and chose poorly, and because of that choice introduced into the human race what theologians call, "original sin," a corrupted condition that still plagues us, trapping us all in the consequences of their decision. The evil they and the devil—not God—chose to introduce into the world is a deadly disease of the soul that brings physical and spiritual death to us all. To make matters worse, everyone has willingly endorsed our first parents' fall. Each of us has helped spread this infectious disease by our own poor choices.

> **We need God and his love, because we simply cannot grasp his unexplained and unexplainable answers.**

Another consequence of sin is that our world is now a dangerous place for victims as well as perpetrators. We have all lost our innocence. However, none of us lost it when we became crooks, or cops, or those caught in the middle. The truth is that we all lost our innocence when we were conceived. We are all victims and we are all perpetrators. This is the ugly reality of original sin (read Psalm 51:5). Only the holy blood of Jesus Christ, God's Son, can cure us of the eternal consequences of our corruption. Only he can heal our fatal infection and restore our lost innocence.

Tragedy and evil exist today because of the devil's deception and humanity's choice. However, knowing the history and the theology of the Fall does little to comfort us when we are forced to cope with the stark realities of the street. For example, it does Widow Jones no good to know her husband was killed by a drunk driver because God created us with dignity and made us humans instead of robots. It gives her no comfort to hear that God gives us a real ability to choose between good and evil actions, with all the consequences that follow those choices. And, it leaves her cold to hear that we chose poorly and are thus locked into an endless cycle of sin and suffering on this earth. These things are all true, but they provide no comfort for Widow Jones as she cries at her kitchen table.

What Widow Jones needs, what we all need in the face of tragedy and evil, is not mere explanation, but comfort and assurance. In tragic situations, we don't need a spiritual lecture. We need a spiritual friend instead. We need God and his love, because we simply cannot grasp his unexplained and unexplainable answers. In Bible times, people occasionally asked God a "why" question, but he did not always give a "why" answer. Job asked God why, but God did not explain.

He simply asserted that he was God. In an amazing display of faith, Job clung to God despite his doubt and despair (Job 19:25-27). Even Jesus, hanging on the cross, asked according to his human nature, "My God, my God, why have you abandoned me?" (Matthew 27:46). God gave his own Son no answer, but instead left him to die the most horrible death in history. However, Jesus, too, trusted his Father's love, and in trusting him, saved us. The most amazing truth of time and eternity is the fact that Jesus took our evil and tragedy, our "Why have you abandoned me?" reality upon himself, so that we could be rescued from Satan, who held us at gunpoint in the hostage situation of our human condition.

Although God does not devote much time to answering the "why" questions in Scripture, he does spend a lot of time talking about the "who" answers. For instance, he spends a lot of time explaining *who* he is and *who* we are. These clues provide the answer we really need from God. They all come together in God's love and our trust. Let me illustrate this truth with a story.

> **Just as God's mind is greater than ours, so too is his love.**

When my youngest daughter was four years old, we went on a family vacation to California. If, before our trip, I had tried to explain to her the route we would take, our schedule, and our activities, she would not have comprehended any of it with her four-year-old mind. She did not have a developed concept of time and was not capable of translating concrete maps into abstract ideas of travel. She wasn't even fully sure she knew what the word "vacation" meant!

So, my wife and I didn't try to explain these details to her. Instead, we spent our time talking generally about the fun we would have on our trip. We showed her how excited we were and she also became excited. The key to her confident excitement was not her knowledge about the trip, but her knowledge of her parents. She knew who we were. She knew who she was. She knew that we loved her and that she could trust us. And, she knew that this vacation was going to be a good thing simply because we said so. In effect, she put her hand in ours and came along, not really knowing where the trip would lead, but knowing that she could trust us that it would be a great ride. And it was.

This simple story may show in some small way the truth about what we can and should know about the deepest questions of life. In Isaiah 55:8-9, God tells us, "'My thoughts are not your thoughts, and my ways are not your ways,' declares the Lord. 'Just as the heavens are higher than the earth, so are my ways higher than your ways, and my thoughts are higher than your thoughts.'" The gulf between the mind of our heavenly Father and his earthly children is much wider than the gulf between the mind of human parent and child. How can we expect God to explain to us the "why" of our grand journey with him, when we cannot even explain a trip to California to our four-year old? How could God possibly explain to us, in words and ideas we could understand, the why of the universe? We can only receive his simple message of *who* he is and *what* he does for us, so we can trust his love. Only then can we trust him with the unanswerable questions. This is the key to what we really need in facing evil and tragedy. We need *his* love. We need *him*. *He* is the key.

Just as God's mind is greater than ours, so too is his love. After all, which one of us would willingly sacrifice our child to save a perpetrator? Yet, this is exactly what our heavenly Father has done for us. In love, he gave his only Son to save an entire race of perpetrators—including you and me! Because of his love, God allowed evil and tragedy to kill his own dear Son. The deepest question of all time is not, "Why does God allow evil and tragedy," but, "Why did Jesus die for you and me?" I don't know why he loves us so, but I'm glad he does (Ephesians 2:1-10)!

In trust, we can grasp God's love. In love, we can grasp his hand. In grasping his hand, we can walk with him in peace and joy on our journey. And then, someday, we will go to that good place where his road leads, and there discover, like a child now grown, that it was really not we who held his hand, but he who always held ours.

Father,

In all honesty, I confess to you that sometimes I wonder how in the world you can allow some of the things I see day in and day out. Many times I don't know the reasons why, but I do know who you are and who we are. We've got some real problems on this planet and we definitely need your help. Thanks for sending your Son in the uniform of human flesh to rescue us from the sin and sorrow I see all around. I pray that the people I deal with every day will turn to you in their sin and misery, so that they can experience the peace you want to bring to every-

one, but force on no one. Bring that peace to me, too, Father, as I wrestle with these troubling realities that weary me, so that I can be part of the solution and not part of the problem. In Jesus' name I pray, let it be so, Amen.

"O God, you are my God. At dawn I search for you. My soul searches for you. My body longs for you in a dry, parched land where there is no water. So I look for you in the holy place to see your power and your glory. My lips will praise you because your mercy is better than life itself. So I will thank you as long as I live. I will lift up my hands to pray in your name. You satisfy my soul with the richest foods. My mouth will sing your praise with joyful lips. As I lie on my bed, I remember you. Through the long hours of the night, I think about you. You have been my help. In the shadow of your wings, I sing joyfully. My soul clings to you. Your right hand supports me." *Psalm 63:1-8*

"Seek the Lord while he may be found. Call on him while he is near. Let wicked people abandon their ways. Let evil people abandon their thoughts. Let them return to the Lord, and he will show compassion to them. Let them return to our God, because he will freely forgive them. 'My thoughts are not your thoughts, and my ways are not your ways,' declares the Lord. 'Just as the heavens are higher than the earth, so my ways are higher than your ways, and my thoughts are higher than your thoughts.' 'Rain and snow come down from the sky. They do not go back again until they water the earth. They make it sprout and grow so that it produces seed for farmers and food for people to eat. My word, which comes from my mouth, is like the rain and snow. It will not come back to me without results, but it will accomplish whatever I want and achieve whatever I send it to do.'" *Isaiah 55:6-12*

A COP CHRISTMAS CAROL
(WITH APOLOGIES TO CHARLES DICKENS)

IKE DUNCAN FELT HIS BLOOD PRESSURE GO UP again. Now this in addition to having to work Christmas Eve. Bah, humbug. He tossed the subpoena back in his box as he adjusted and snapped the last keeper on his belt.

"Always on my days off," he grumped, mentally crossing off his planned getaway. He grabbed his gear and headed for briefing. As he rounded a corner, Sanchez, the new kid in District Two, almost ran him over on his way to the locker room.

"Hey, 'Dunk 'Em!'" Sanchez exclaimed. "Gonna kick some and take some names tonight?"

"I shoot hit and run suspects, Amigo. Stay out of my way," Mike responded. "And, don't use my Christian name until you at least get off probation. It's 'Mr. Duncan,' 'Officer Duncan,' or, preferably, 'All-Supreme Ruler of Rookies' to you." Duncan's nickname, a memorial to a long ago foot pursuit of a burglar into an apartment complex swimming pool, irritated him, especially when taken in vain by a squeaky academy graduate who probably hadn't even been born back then.

At briefing, Sergeant Cheryl Washington delivered her typical crisp monologue. As she spoke, Mike reflected briefly on all the changes in the Department since he joined after Vietnam. He remembered when women and minorities in his agency were a rarity. He himself had never wanted to promote, but it bugged him that Washington, who was both female *and* black, made Sergeant so quickly. He credited her gender and race for the promotion. But, his basic honesty forced him to admit, even if only to himself, that she was a competent and fair supervisor. And she had her hands full as a single mom. There was no doubt that she had to put up with a lot, including Michael Duncan. But, he told himself that if she wanted to play with the big boys, she had to play by big boys' rules; no breaks. For the first time since coming to work, he smiled.

"...and so B.O.L. for that suspected vehicle and don't pull a John Wayne if you spot it. Wait for your backup." Washington set the "Patrol" clipboard aside, and picked up, "Memos and Directives."

"Only one new edict from on high," Washington scanned. "The Captain has been receiving citizen complaints about patrol cars driving too fast on McPherson and he reminds us to watch our speed per departmental response and pursuit policies."

Mike made a face. "Are those the same concerned citizens who complained about our slow response time about a month ago, and the Captain jacked us up about it? McPherson is the main artery to the west side gang-bangers and we're short on people, as usual, thanks to the concerned citizens of our fair community. Duncan's Theory of Relativity: too much space and not enough time. Beam me to the west end, Scotty, so I can protect and serve our brothers of color. Cap can't have it both ways, Sergeant." He slowly rolled out the word, "Sergeant." "I think maybe the bars on his collar are pinching off his carotids, or maybe it's the altitude and lack of oxygen on Admin. What do you think, Sergeant?"

Washington sighed, "Thanks for the enlightened commentary, Officer Duncan. Just try and slow down a bit, okay folks? You won't help anybody if you T-bone someone en route to a call. And, Mike, I know you are the Master of Malicious Compliance, so let me also remind you that this gem of wisdom from the Captain does not excuse you from your responsibility to promptly descend from your monogrammed throne at Dunkin' Donuts if you get an in-progress on the west side."

"Yes sir, ma'am, and I'll be sure to stop at the pharmacy and pick up your hormone pills, Ms. Washington."

Christmas Past

Duncan flipped the keys off the board and went out to his squad car to run through his vehicle inspection. With the advent of AIDS and other delightful diseases, he was paranoid about cuts and punctures and he took extra care checking the back seat for stashed weapons and contraband, especially needles. Vehicle check complete, he then placed the Remington 870 into its shotgun rack, pulled on the lock to make sure it was properly closed, and double-checked the safety. As he arranged his computer, briefcase, flashlight, clipboard, and the other miscellaneous odds

"Just two more years to retirement," he thought grimly to himself.

and ends of patrol work in the front seat, he longed for the simpler times and larger cars of former years. The new cars did not have enough room and twenty-eight years of patrol work had taken a toll. His lower back ached from more than a quarter of a century of wearing pounds of equipment and sitting on broken-down seat springs. He had partial disabilities in both knees from job-related injuries and he also had a blood pressure problem. He tried to stay in shape, but it got harder as he got older. "Just two more years to retirement," he thought grimly to himself.

As he radioed "in-service" and hit the road, he continued his thoughts of the past. He remembered the years of boredom mixed with fear, anger, disgust, and endless paperwork. He remembered what he called his "boy scout years," when he had first volunteered for the Marines and then later joined the police department. He had wanted to make a difference and he admitted to himself that

He had wanted to make a difference and he admitted to himself that the hero fantasy had also played its part. Although he still thought of himself as a good cop, he knew he was really just hanging on till he could maximize his retirement. He looked forward to pulling the pin.

the hero fantasy had also played its part. Then he had run up against the Real World—a place where Truth, Justice and the

American Way do not always rule. Although he still thought of himself as a good cop, he knew he was really just hanging on till he could maximize his retirement. He looked forward to pulling the pin.

He recalled other changes the years had wrought in himself. With a pang of conscience, he again recognized that his loss of innocence had also made victims of those around him, especially his family. Beth, his high school sweetheart, had finally given up on their marriage after sticking with him through Nam and his first few years as a cop. She had moved and remarried a long time ago. It wasn't much better with the kids. They had grown up so fast and, although he loved them more than life itself, he realized that he did not even really know them. He was so wrapped up in the culture of his work when they were little. Now, when he recognized the locust years and wanted to somehow make up for them, his kids had moved on with their own lives.

> **Outside of police work, Krueger had no hobbies, no interests, and no relationships.**

Duncan stopped for the changing light, instead of running it like he usually did. He tilted the rearview mirror and looked at the gray hair and into the eyes, and he saw the burned-out dinosaur he used to mock as a hot-dog rookie looking back at him.

Christmas Future

"10, 12, you clear?" Duncan picked up the mike and gave an "Affirm," and his next location. Five minutes later Rogers pulled up next to his driver's window. Dean was Mike's best friend in the department. They went through the Academy together and stood by one another and saved one another's bacon more than once in the years since.

"Hiya, Mike, you goin' to the funeral?"

"Don't think so, got plans that day. It won't matter to Karl, anyway, will it?"

Both officers were quiet for a minute. Karl Krueger was a veteran officer who had retired about a year previously after 30 years on the force, but who periodically came down to the station after that. Mike always felt uneasy watching Karl wander around in civilian clothes, looking like an aging, lost child. Karl's whole life had been the work. He divorced years ago and lived alone. His children never spoke to him. Outside of police work, Krueger had no hobbies, no interests, and no relationships. Mike remembered that Karl had always talked up his retirement, but when the time came, he just didn't know how. When his career ended, so did his life—the heart attack was just a formality. Suddenly, Mike felt a winter chill coming from a place other than his open window.

Finally, Dean look at him and said, "Oh well, you know what ol' Cruel Krueg always said…"

"Yeah…'Life's a bummer, and then you die.'"

Christmas Present

After Duncan booked a drunk whose attitude demanded jail rather than detox, Dispatch radioed Mike to assist with traffic control at Saint Michael's Lutheran Church. The church was hosting its annual Living Nativity, an increasingly popular drive-past event. Mike frowned at the radio. He didn't like the idea of leaving his warm car to stand on a cold street and duck looky-loo traffic. As he pulled up to the front lawn of the church, he shook his head. They had actually added live animals this year. "Oh well, time to freeze," he thought.

> **Life's pretty messed up sometimes, isn't it?"**

Later, as he directed the dwindling number of vehicles past the church, he happened to glance over at the "Saint Michael's" on the church sign. Michael, the name of the patron angel of peace officers and his own name, too. How appropriate, he thought, but wouldn't it be nice for the angel to come direct his own traffic? Just then, as he stepped back to get a better look at the sign, he tripped over the curb and almost fell. At the same time, a minivan blew by the place where he had been standing just a moment before. "Michael to the rescue," he thought after a startled moment. "I guess I've given him a few gray hairs, too."

A small boy's voice came from the corner, "Hey, Mister Police Officer, you'd better look out for those cars!"

"Thanks, kid, don't know what I'd do without your help." Duncan looked over to where the boy was standing and noticed that he was dressed in a shepherd's costume and was on crutches. "You part of the show? I thought a shepherd was supposed to carry a staff—not crutches. And, how come you're not with your sheep?" Duncan looked over to where two forlorn-looking sheep were staked out by the manger.

"I came over to say 'hi.' My name's Tim. What's yours?"

Mike smiled. "That's good. Tiny Tim, complete with crutches. Well, Tiny Tim, my name's Michael. Glad to meet you." Duncan retained a soft spot for children.

"Michael, like the name of our church. Are you a saint, too?"

"Not hardly, Tiny Tim. What happened to your leg?"

"We got in an accident last year. Daddy died. They had to operate on my leg again a couple of months ago, but I get the cast off in a week."

Duncan stopped smiling as Tim continued, "The police arrested the man in the other car. He didn't get hurt. They said he wasn't supposed to be driving 'cause he was drunk."

Figures, thought Mike. The drunks always seemed to have their own guardian angel. He would have to ask God about that someday, if he got the chance...

"Well, Tim, sorry about your dad. Life's pretty messed up sometimes, isn't it?"

"Yeah, I guess, but that's why Jesus came—to fix it!" Tim beamed at Duncan. "That's why I wanted to be the shepherd boy. I want people to remember about Jesus coming and fixing things."

"Seems he missed the boat on fixing it for your dad, though," Duncan responded, and then mentally kicked himself for taking a potshot at this little boy's faith. He asked himself if he had to be a jerk all the time.

Tim never missed a beat, "Oh, no!" he declared. "Jesus fixed it for my dad, too. Daddy trusted Jesus and we're going to all be together in heaven forever someday. No more accidents and bad stuff there! You know Jesus, too, don't you, Michael?"

> **"God, I'm tired,"**
> **he murmured, and**
> **then realized that**
> **he had just prayed**
> **his first real prayer**
> **in years.**

It wasn't often that Duncan didn't know what to say. He looked at Tim, then he looked at the sign in front of the church, and then he looked at the cross on top of the church. He tried to remember back when he was a child like Tim and he couldn't, not really. He remembered some of the Bible stories, but the knowing part, the happy faith part, was missing now.

"I would like to know, to believe. But, Tim, it's pretty hard when you've seen the stuff I've seen and done the stuff I've done."

"That's okay, Michael. That's why Jesus came for you, too. He came for everybody. He'll fix the hole in your soul. That's what Mom says. He's the Prince of Peace. Hey, you goin' to the candlelight service?"

"I'm going home..." Mike paused. What home? Home to a six-pack and TV in a lousy apartment? Home to nobody and nothing? He remembered last year at Christmas when he got drunk at home alone and briefly considered eating his gun. He had never told anyone about that, not even Dean. The irony overwhelmed him; no peace for this peace officer. What did preachers call it, an epistle? No, an epiphany. Whatever it was, he was having one now. "God, I'm tired," he murmured, and then realized that he had just prayed his first real prayer in years. His second prayer, more fervent than the first, came a moment later. "Lord, I don't know if it's too late, but please don't let me be another Krueger."

Mike put his hand on Tim's shoulder. "You think they'd let me in your church, Tiny Tim? The roof might cave in."

Tim smiled up at him. "It's got a strong roof and they gotta let you in; it's your church, too. It's even got your name on it! You can meet my mom. She gets off from the hospital pretty soon. She's an R.N.," he said proudly.

Mike smiled back. Cops and nurses. Well...he'd have to check with Sergeant Washington if this was going to happen. He didn't have time to go back to the station and change before the service started, but at least his shift would be over. He went to his car, picked up the cell phone, and called the Sergeant.

"Hey, Sarge, it's Duncan. Umm, I got an invite to go to the midnight candlelight service at Saint Mike's, and I was wondering if I could go off duty here and bring the squad car back afterwards."

He felt something he had not experienced in years, a feeling like home.

There was a long pause on the other end. Then he heard Washington say, "You're telling me you want to go to church? Did I hear you right, Officer Duncan?"

"Yeah, Sarge, you heard me right. I think I'm overdue."

"Well, it's okay with me, but before you go, you should probably know that Saint Michael's is my church, too, and I'm bringing my kids to that service tonight. Are you sure you want to be seen with me, Officer Duncan?"

Mike took a deep breath. "Look, Cheryl. I've been riding your case from day one. I was wrong and I apologize. I don't know how to explain all this right now, this is new to me, but I need some things to be different. Anyway, I don't mind sitting next to an over-achiever, rookie sergeant like you, if you don't mind sitting next to a knee-jerk, reactionary, prejudiced, burn-out case like me. What do you say?"

"Well, Mike, this is new to me, too. But, let me pick myself up off the floor and dust myself off and I'll see you at church." They hung up.

Just then Tim brought his mother up to the car. A very attractive mother, Mike noted. I guess some things won't change, he thought. But, for once in your life, be a gentleman about it, he instructed himself.

"Hi, Michael. I'm Rebecca. I hope Tim hasn't been bothering you too much. He tells me he invited you to church tonight." She took her hand out of her glove and extended it.

He took her hand in his and her warmth radiated through him. "Yes, ma'am. Hope you don't mind. Sorry about having to go in uniform, but I don't have time to go to the station and change."

Rebecca looked him over carefully and smiled. Mike fidgeted with embarrassment before her. He felt as if those pretty blue eyes were looking right through him and examining that hole in his soul, but he liked the feeling.

"That's okay, Michael. I've seen uniforms in the ER and I'm still wearing mine, too. It's good to have you come worship Jesus with us."

During the service, as Mike lit his candle from the one Tim was holding and passed the flame on to Rebecca, he looked across the aisle at an amazed Cheryl Washington and smiled. The roof hadn't caved in and, maybe this Christmas Eve would usher in a new trick for this old dog's life. He felt something he had not experienced in years, a feeling like home. God bless us every one, he thought. He opened the hymn book and began to sing, "Silent night, holy night..."

AN ISLAND OF HOPE

SERGEANT DENNIS CONROY, A LAW ENFORCEMENT
veteran with the St. Paul, Minnesota Police Department,
is also a competent and dedicated police psychologist who
devotes himself to the welfare of his fellow officers. He has
written a book, *Officers at Risk*, in which he describes many of
the personal problems peace officers face because of their
work. It is his painful observation that the life of a peace officer is a litany of loss, and that the most significant and oft-
repeated loss that officers express is a "loss of innocence." Ask
a rookie officer why he or she entered law enforcement. Their
typical answer is they want to "help people." But, when older
officers are asked why they are cops, they often give less idealistic answers. They give economic answers such as, "job
security, paycheck, hanging on until I retire," or they give
practical answers such as, "no other options."

What happens to change idealistic young officers into
cynical veterans? According to Sergeant Conroy, a "loss of
innocence" occurs. When officers begin their career, they
usually have an idealized view of the human condition. They
are the bright-eyed, but near-sighted product of our society,
which boldly proclaims our potential, while masking our mistakes and our mortality. But, after a few years on the job,

those same officers carry a view abruptly sharpened by experience to 20/20 vision. They now see the world as it truly is—warts and all. They see case after painful case of greedy grubbing for power and position and they endure the fallout of rampant and worsening victimization, injustice, hypocrisy, tragedy, cowardice and corruption. They see the reality that, too often, there is no redress of grievance in this world. They often conclude that there is *no island of hope* for a world drowning in a rising sea of sin and suffering. Their misplaced faith in humanity, including faith in their own ability to change things for the better, is shattered. Rather than firmly placing their faith where it belongs, on the foundation of God's Word, they often become spiritual descendents of the "Lost Generation" who became so disillusioned following the human horrors of World War I. Hope sinks with innocence.

All of this leads me to ask the very important question, "Is there an island of hope?" You probably already know that you don't generate your own hope. You know your hope doesn't come from advancement, political gain or even recognition for valor because you know that, although enjoyable, those are temporary achievements. You may examine your personal life and your relationships and find little or no hope in those places. In reality, your hope can only have one true Source and that is the God who made you and protects you on your beat every day of your life. If you are in the place of cynicism and fatigue, take a moment to pray.

Ask God to renew your hope, to stand before you in everything you do and to remind you that he alone gives you purpose and power—he is your island of hope.

God,

Sometimes I look around at the ocean of sin and sorrow that surrounds me and I just get tired all over. The world wants to drag me down into the deep, but you are my rock, my island in the eye of the hurricane and, because I stand on you, I will never be blown away by that storm or drowned by that sea. Renew my strength so that I not only stand, but fly like an eagle through the wind and above the waves of this life. Thanks and praise to you, Lord God! Your presence is tried and your promises are true,

Amen.

"I love you, O Lord, my strength. The Lord is my rock and my fortress and my Savior, my God, my rock in whom I take refuge, my shield, and the strength of my salvation, my stronghold. The Lord should be praised. I called on him, and I was saved from my enemies. The ropes of death had become tangled around me. The torrents of destruction had overwhelmed me. The ropes of the grave had surrounded me. The clutches of death had confronted me. I called on the Lord in my distress. I cried to my God for help. He heard my voice from his temple, and my cry for help reached his ears. *Psalm 18:1-6*

"Don't you know? Haven't you heard? The eternal God, the Lord, the Creator of the ends of the earth, doesn't grow tired or become weary. His understanding is beyond reach. He gives strength to those who grow tired and increases the strength of those who are weak. Even young people grow tired and become weary, and young men will stumble and fall. Yet, the strength of those who wait with hope in the Lord will be renewed. They will soar on wings like eagles. They will run and won't become weary. They will walk and won't grow tired." *Isaiah 40:28-31*

YOUR WEAPONS ON THE
SPIRITUAL STREET

"SO THEN, TAKE YOUR STAND! FASTEN TRUTH AROUND your waist like a belt. Put on God's approval as your breastplate. Put on your shoes so that you are ready to spread the Good News that gives peace. In addition to all these, take the Christian faith as your shield. With it you can put out all the flaming arrows of the evil one. Also take salvation as your helmet and the word of God as the sword that the Spirit supplies. Ephesians 6:14-17

OLD, NEW, AND
RENEWED CENTURIONS

THE BIBLE IS FULL OF COP STORIES AND REFERENCES to law enforcement. For instance, although Christ serves as the ultimate example of a peace officer, Roman centurions can also be compared to officers in today's society. Centurions were Roman soldiers who were officers in charge of one hundred men. Roman soldiers and the centurions who supervised them exercised a military role, as well as a civil law enforcement role. Without exception, centurions in the New Testament are portrayed in a favorable light. They were models of faith and virtue. The following verses highlight a bit about their lives:

"When Jesus went to Capernaum, a Roman army officer came to beg him for help. The officer said, 'Sir, my servant is lying at home paralyzed and in terrible pain.' Jesus said to him, 'I'll come to heal him.' The officer responded, 'Sir, I don't deserve to have you come into my house. But just give a command, and my servant will be healed. As you know, I'm in a chain of command and have soldiers at my command. I tell one of them, 'Go!' and he goes, and another, 'Come!' and he comes. I tell my servant, 'Do this!' and he does it.' Jesus was amazed when he heard this. He said to those who were following him, 'I can guarantee this truth: I haven't found faith as great as this in anyone in Israel.'... Jesus told the officer, 'Go! What you believed will be done for you.' And at that moment the servant was healed." *Matthew 8:5-13*

In the Bible, centurions model compassion, humility, submission to proper authority, faith, philanthropy, piety, devotion to duty, integrity, unselfish service, good reputation, fairness, hospitality and wisdom. Today, the most respected peace officers in our nation demonstrate the same personal characteristics. Officers today have even been called, "new centurions."

Take his hand— he's already reached for yours.

One of our greatest lessons for officers from historical accounts involves the centurion Cornelius and is found in the book of Acts, chapters 10 and 11. Cornelius, like the other centurions mentioned in Scripture, was a peace officer of integrity and faith, but he recognized that he still needed—as we all do—spiritual "backup" from history's ultimate Peace Officer, Jesus Christ. Cornelius became a renewed centurion by the power of Peter's teaching. As a result, Cornelius received the protection and peace of Christ for all eternity. Like Cornelius, the centurion of old, new centurions need to be renewed centurions.

In your community, you face situations everyday that are incomprehensible to civilians. You see the worst of the world. In spite of this and, even better, because of this, the call of Christ to become a renewed centurion remains the same for you as it was for Cornelius and the other Roman centurions who are shown as spiritual examples. He extends his hand to you every day—for comfort from tears, for relief from stress, for calm on a difficult day and, most importantly, for grace and peace throughout all eternity.

Take his hand—he's already reached for yours.

Jesus Christ, Son of God,

Thank you for the example of the centurions of old in Scripture. Help me, as a new centurion, to be a renewed centurion in your kingdom. Help me to follow the example of faith and life set by those peace officers. Help me remember that, if they could maintain faith and integrity and hope despite the corruption and evil all around them, then by your power and strength, I can, too. Thanks for being my centurion, my peace officer,

Amen.

"A person's steps are directed by the Lord, and the Lord delights in his way. When he falls, he will not be thrown down headfirst because the Lord holds on to his hand." *Psalm 37:23-24*

"Come to me, all who are tired from carrying heavy loads, and I will give you rest. Place my yoke over your shoulders, and learn from me, because I am gentle and humble. Then you will find rest for yourselves because my yoke is easy and my burden is light." *Matthew 11:28-30*

"Look, I'm standing at the door and knocking. If anyone listens to my voice and opens the door, I'll come in and we'll eat together." *Revelation 3:20*

DRAWING THE LINE

A WHILE BACK I WAS LISTENING TO THE NEWS ON THE drive home from my office and heard our now former vice president swearing in the newly elected congress. He finished leading the oath of office with these words, "...so help me God." As I listened to those noble words, I reflected ruefully on a conversation I had with an officer who works in his department's professional standards division. He told me - sadly - that his city had quietly eliminated that historic phrase from the oath its new officers take. In the same conversation, he remarked on how difficult it is to find good people to recruit into law enforcement today. Seems some folks today do not have the same commitment, values, and integrity they used to have. Go figure...

I wonder. Is there some person sucking at the trough of the public payroll in that city who has defined his or her duty as divorcing that apparently offensive phrase, "so help me God," once and for all from their officers' official vocabulary and character? Maybe that person figures, "Hey, if we can just eliminate God from the playing field, our city will be utopia and we will finally be able to find those good officers our professional standards division is looking for." After all, God just gets in the way of professionalism, right...?

Congress may need God's help, but our officers sure don't, right...?

Not long ago, I saw some news footage of a presidential swearing-in ceremony, and watched as our new president placed his hand on a Bible, like every chief executive of our land does every four years. I find no lack of irony in the fact that we expect our chief law enforcement officer to place his hand on a Bible, but in this same country, there are law enforcement agencies that prohibit the on-site donation of free Bibles to officers who want them. I find additional irony in the fact that one of those restrictive agencies has a small version of the Statue of Liberty in front of it, complete with a sentiment about upholding the faith of our country's fathers, "who made possible the freedom of these United States." What faith, may I ask? What freedom? Freedom *of* religion, or freedom *from* religion, enforced by state decree, and thus no freedom at all? Seems like the only publicly permissible faith and freedom today is politically correct post-modern secular humanism, with even the "humanism" portion of the equation in jeopardy because of our devaluation of human life and our personification (sometimes deification) of Mother Earth and the critters

> **I find no lack of irony in the fact that we expect our chief law enforcement officer to place his hand on a Bible, but there are agencies that prohibit the donation of free Bibles to officers who want them.**

on it. Seems the only people who can be publicly picked on today with impunity are fat people and Christians (I guess overweight Christians are in trouble).

Our society's modern religion is "Tolerance," which, in this case, means tolerating anything and everything, *except* folks who believe in absolutes. We are absolutely, positively intolerant of those people. Today, you are not allowed to believe *something*. You must believe *everything*—contradictions, muddle-headedness, error, and evil notwithstanding. No wonder our society's children too often have been dumbed down to believe *nothing*. This bonehead propaganda by definition sets up Christianity as Public Enemy Number One, because historic Christianity is the most visible religious target in our society. It dares proclaim right is right and wrong is wrong, and Jesus Christ is the Way, the Truth, and the Life, and *no one* comes to the Father except by him (John 14:6). Never mind if Christianity is true. It is *offensive*, and thus—again note the irony—it is not to be tolerated. Our modern "Tolerance" religion is not just dumb. It is hypocritical.

It is true we have a diverse society that, properly, promotes liberty and justice for all. This is why we have a Bill of Rights. It is also no accident that the first of these amendments talks about freedom of religion and freedom of speech: "Congress shall make no law respecting an establishment of religion, or prohibiting the free exercise thereof; or abridging the freedom of speech, or of the press, or the right of the people peaceably to assemble, and to petition the government for a redress of grievances."

Just because we jealously, and once again properly, defend the rights of diverse people with diverse opinions, we need not

stand up and cheer for every opinion, or hold that every opinion is equally true and good. The First Amendment guards our
right to state *publicly* that certain things are true and good, and
certain other things are false and bad. We need not reach an
impossible-to-reach consensus before we can speak. We have
the *right* in this country to stand up publicly and speak, or sing,
or pray our conscience. So, like the Nike commercial says, just
do it. Don't let anyone shout you down or intimidate you into
silence, even under color of authority. We must obey God, not
man, and our Declaration of Independence and our Con-
stitution give us the right, and furthermore the *duty*, to do so.

Government is not supposed to establish a state-approved
religion, but neither is it to interfere with the free exercise of
religion. "In God We Trust" on our money, "so help me God"
in our oaths of office, "one nation, under God" in our pledge
of allegiance, or our president's hand on a Bible is *not* establishing a state mandated religion. It is simply acknowledging
that God exists, and we as a society must honor him and his
principles to remain a free and just nation.

As another example, prohibitions against the religious
activities of chaplains, unless those activities are a clear
impediment to the necessary functioning of an agency, are to
be avoided. In one properly balanced application of this principle, chaplains should not proselytize officers, but certainly
they may share their beliefs when asked (this is a good biblical principle, by the way, see 1 Peter 3:15-16). Further, when
chaplains speak publicly, they need to be careful not to repre-
sent their religious beliefs as an official departmental position,
but neither are they required to boil down their beliefs into a
useless politically acceptable stew.

A common issue facing police chaplains especially is the issue of public prayer. Is it appropriate, or even legal, for a chaplain to offer a distinctive public prayer, such as a Jewish prayer, or a Christian prayer offered in Jesus' name? The whole point of our right to free expression in this country is the principle that each one of us is allowed to define for ourselves our own faith, and to publicly express that faith. This does not imply government endorsement of any religion, but is an opportunity for government to exercise its responsibility as a guarantor of free speech. The solution is not so-called "inclusive" prayer, because, in fact, no such prayer exists. Somebody's beliefs will *always* be excluded no matter how many theologians and lawyers become involved, and someone will always be offended on religious, if not legal, grounds. Rather, as citizens, we should all respect one another's right to pray as we wish, and stand up and cheer that right as a hallmark of our country's greatness, even if religiously we have heartburn over the content of that prayer. Thus, for instance, I do not demand a Jewish Rabbi pray a Christian prayer, and he does not demand I pray a Jewish prayer. Rather, we both guard the other's right to freely pray as we wish, according to our conscience, and rejoice that in this country, at least, we have the right to do so.

> **The whole point...is the principle that each one of us is allowed to define for ourselves our own faith, and to publicly express that faith.**

Our prayers are the unavoidably deepest expression of our heart; our beliefs. To deny our heart reflects neither integrity nor legal requirement. The solution to religious diversity is not an amalgamated prayer, which only satisfies those who are comfortable with fuzzy theological boundaries. Rather, we should each pray according to our convictions, and it is not the State's responsibility or anyone else's to dictate how we express them.

As a practical matter, I have observed that what is and is not allowed in police agencies is often determined by governmental executive leadership, not by statute or court decision. This leadership, in turn, is often dictated to by political, philosophical, or even personal considerations. Using our earlier example, the Gideon Bible Society tells me there is no legal

> **Our prayers are the unavoidably deepest expression of our heart; our beliefs.**

prohibition against the distribution of Bibles at police departments, but that distribution is discretionary on the part of the agency head. The difference is not statutory law, case law, or even the Supreme Court. The difference is the leadership of the agencies or governments involved. These leaders are sometimes dictated to by political pressure, not legal requirement. Even legal requirement is often open to interpretation by the executive branch of government. Too often, legalities improperly cloak philosophical, political, and even personal purposes, and are sometimes misunderstood, misrepresented, or misapplied. The truth is that our courts have given us broad religious freedoms to avoid First Amendment problems.

Obviously, and especially in today's political and moral climate, it takes leaders with some backbone to stand against the "anything goes but absolutes" thinking of today, and for our civil rights. It takes courageous and principled leaders to stand for time-tested beliefs and values.

It is time to draw the line and hold our leaders and ourselves accountable, "so help us God."

A REAL WORD FOR A REAL WORLD

THE BIBLE TELLS ABOUT GOD'S LOVE FOR ALL people—including peace officers (John 3:16-17). Peace officers, like all people, need to listen to God's Word of law and then, by the power of his Spirit, repent of sin and receive the life God offers. With this truth in mind, we need to be careful not to dismiss the Bible as just another ancient and archaic "Code of Hammurabi," suitable maybe for footnoting in a criminal justice class, but not applicable to the real world faced by peace officers. God's Word is not a vague and irrelevant collection of religious writings. The Word is not the outdated and debatable voice of long-dead men. It is the unchanging and unchangeable voice of the Living God, offering law and life to the real world in which we live.

Every Scripture passage is inspired by God.

God,

I thank and praise you for your Father-given, Spirit-inspired, Son-revealing Word. I thank you that your word is the real deal and not some piece of fluff philosophy that gets blown away by the first puff of pressure. Thank you that your word not only paints an accurate picture of the problems we face, but that it also portrays our solution, our Savior, Jesus Christ. Surround me and fill me with your word always, Lord, so that I can walk tall with you in this world. In your name I pray,

Amen.

"God's word is living and active. It is sharper than any two-edged sword and cuts as deep as the place where soul and spirit meet, the place where joints and marrow meet. God's word judges a person's thoughts and intentions." *(Hebrews 4:12).*

"However, continue in what you have learned and found to be true. You know who your teachers were. From infancy you have known the Holy Scriptures. They have the power to give you wisdom so that you can be saved through faith in Christ Jesus. Every Scripture passage is inspired by God. All of them are useful for teaching, pointing out errors, correcting people, and training them for a life that has God's approval. They equip God's servants so that they are completely prepared to do good things." *2 Timothy 3:14-17*

TEN TIPS FOR SPIRITUAL
SURVIVAL AS A PEACE
OFFICER

I N MY LAW ENFORCEMENT CAREER, I HAD OFFICER
safety drilled into me from day one by books, manuals, video-
tapes, "shoot/don't shoot" scenarios, academy instructors, field
training officers, in-service presenters, supervisors, fellow officers and agents, and, ultimately, by my own hard-won experience on the street. I was hammered constantly by the need to
watch my back, watch the suspect's hands, ask the "what if…"
questions, stay alert, blade off, do a proper handcuffing and
search, keep my gun side away from the suspect, and so on.

Cops are trained paranoids, but like the saying goes, "Just
because you're paranoid doesn't necessarily mean no one's out
to get you." Officers understand that in some ways the street
is a battleground much like Vietnam, where soldiers were
sometimes unsure who was a friend and who was a foe and
where they were always on the lookout for booby traps and
ambushes of one sort or another. I once asked a buddy of
mine, to compare his Vietnam War experience with his 30
years of police work. He told me that there were similarities,
but surprised me by saying that, in some ways, being a cop

was tougher. He said that, in Vietnam, no matter how bad things got you always knew your tour would end after a year or so, but in police work the tour never ends. This observation should make every cop pause and pay attention to *all* officer survival issues if he or she wants to last the long haul.

I knew an officer (who shall remain nameless to protect the guilty) who once came upon a middle-of-the-street, free-for-all fisticuffs between a man and a woman. He—properly—called for backup and separated the combatants, but then—improperly—placed the woman in the uncaged back seat of his car, *with* her purse unsearched and *without* handcuffs. The officer then told the male half of the problem to remain at the front of his car while he sat down behind the wheel of his unit, with his back to the woman. When I drove up to this pending fiasco and saw what was *not* happening, I grabbed the woman from the officer's car and passed her over to an accompanying officer. I also grabbed her purse. Inside was a chrome .25 semi-auto Saturday night special. The officer in question turned white when he saw the pistola. I didn't say anything—there was no need. It was a blessing no one got hurt, but it was also too bad the officer did not have the same situational clarity before the fact that he had afterward.

> **In addition to physical risks, officers face threats to their emotional, relational and spiritual lives.**

Sometimes we do not have clarity about life until it is too late. Officers, with all of their training, usually know how to survive on the street. However, just as often, they struggle to survive spiritually. According to research given at a recent police chaplaincy seminar, peace officers are eight times more likely to commit suicide than they are to be murdered in the line of duty. Shocking, isn't it? This statistic emphasizes the troubling truth that officers face more survival issues than just the risks that confront them on the street. In addition to physical risks, officers face threats to their emotional, relational and spiritual lives.

When I was a rookie in the early 1970's, officer survival lessons for my personal life were limited, like the gruff advice of a veteran cop who once told me, "Kid, watch out for booze, broads and bills." Without commenting on the political correctness of this old-timer's observations, let me just say that the threats to our spiritual survival are serious. We need to be equally serious about defeating them. Officers devote a great deal of time and energy addressing threats to survival on the street. Should we not also spend time and energy addressing—and arresting—the threats in our personal lives? Officer spiritual survival calls for a plan of action that is conscious, consistent and comprehensive.

As a peace officer, I carried a list of "10 Tips for Officer Survival," taped inside my metal clipboard. Included in this list were guidelines on watching the suspect's hands, searching a suspect, staying alert, calling for backup, and other common sense tips. These rules were a helpful reminder to always practice good street survival tactics. Likewise, if we are going to survive spiritually, we need to practice God's principles for spiritual survival.

The following tips come straight from the Bible and a lot of hard experience. Some of these tips are the result of lessons learned from my own stupid mistakes. And, they have *all* preserved my marriage, my family and me, despite those mistakes and despite my periodic inconsistency. If they can work for me and for others, they can work for you, too. You will pay a price if you ignore these tips, but you will discover God's strength and peace by following them. Always remember you have God's help whenever you ask for it. I hope you'll keep these tips at hand. I pray they'll inspire you not just to survive, but to conquer in Christ.

1. *Maintain God's situational awareness—avoid your own tunnel vision.* Respect, honor, obey and trust God in all things, even those things you may not understand, such as suffering and evil. (Job 2:9-10; Job 13:15; Job 19:25-27; Proverbs 9:10; Proverbs 16:9).

2. *Know God's law—and your limits.* Always allow God's law to guide you in your personal and professional life, but also understand God's law cannot save you from sin and eternal death. His grace alone does that. Like the great philosopher, Dirty Harry, once said, "A man has got to know his limitations." (Psalm 119:1; Romans 3:19-24).

3. *Use your backup.* The crucifixion of Christ is the only event in human history that meets the need for ultimate justice *and* mercy in an imperfect world. Believe and receive the Ultimate Peace Officer, Jesus Christ, as your Savior and Lord. We are all perpetrators before God because he is perfect and we are not. But Jesus did not come to bust us. Instead, he treats us as victims of sin and self and Satan. He is the holy Son of God, yet he willingly came from heaven, took on the uniform of human flesh and worked the beat of this world. By

his death on the cross, Jesus stepped between history's ultimate bad guy, Satan, and us, the perpetrators and victims. He took the bullet of eternal death that was aimed at all of us. He rescued us from our hostage situation of sin, death and damnation. He rose again and lives to give us faith and hope and love and peace. Don't play John Wayne. You protect and serve others, but who ultimately protects and serves you? Let Jesus be your backup. (Isaiah 9:6; Isaiah 53; Matthew 4:1-11; Luke 23:33-34; John 14:27; Romans 5:6-10).

> **You protect and serve others, but who ultimately protects and serves you?**

4. *Keep your balance.* Don't take your home problems to work, and don't take your work problems home, either. Let God's law and justice, seasoned by His love, guide your professional life. Let God's love and forgiveness, seasoned by His law, guide your personal life. (Proverbs 16:7,12; Matthew 9:9-13, 18:21-35, 23:23-24)

5. *Train like you fight—fight like you train.* Regularly attend a church that preaches the Bible, promotes a proper balance of law and Gospel and practices prayer. Get involved! Research shows that regular church attendees who practice their faith may not be immune from life's problems, but they *are* less likely to be overcome by those problems. (Acts 2:42; Hebrews 10:25)

6. *Stay in shape—work out with your partners.* Find at least one or two fellow Christians to encourage you

and hold you accountable to a consistent, spiritually integrated life. Meet with them regularly for Bible study and prayer. (Galatians 6:1-2; Ephesians 4:29-32; 1 Thessalonians 5:11)

7. *Maintain and use your tools.* Spend daily devotional time in Bible study, reflection and prayer. Rely on the strength of God's promises to sustain you when you are under the stress of Satan's pressure. These practices will keep you spiritually strong and situationally aware. (Ephesians 6:10-18)

8. *Get your rest.* We all suffer stress or crash and burn on occasion. Know what the signs are. Know when to take a break. Know where to go to ask for help. Know how to relax in healthy ways. Know who to go to. Take care of you and yours physically, emotionally, relationally, and spiritually. (Genesis 2:1-3; Psalm 91:1-2; Luke 10:38-42)

> **"Do good cop work, but avoid being a cop."**

9. *Watch the suspect's hands.* Go home. Spend time with your family and friends away from the trappings of work. Enjoy the good things of life as blessings from God, but don't be a slave to any vice or get trapped by your toys. Avoid driving yourself into debt so that you have to scoop up every ounce of extra duty, which really only adds to your tax burden and work stress. Socialize and be friendly with your co-workers, but stay clear of a harmful after-hours lifestyle and harmful relationships. (John 14:27; 1 John 2:15-17; Romans 13:8-14; Proverbs 22:7; Ephesians 5:15-6:4; 1 Peter 5:8)

10. *Just do it—don't be it.* Take off your game face when you take off your uniform at the end of the shift. You may survive physically in "condition yellow" on a 24/7 basis (although you will probably die prematurely from a stress-related illness or disease), but you *will* wind up lonely and depressed if you cannot leave the hyper-vigilant, intolerant, legalistic, defensive, suspicious, controlling attitude at work. Like my friend, Sgt. Denny Conroy, says, "Do good cop work, but avoid *being* a cop." Be family, be a friend and be a child of God instead. In a happy irony, you will also be a better cop if you follow this advice. Understand that, at the end of your day, at the end of your career and at the end of your life, the most important thing is the love of God and the love of those you love. Relationships are ultimately more important than a role. (1 Corinthians 13; Mark 12:28-34)

Research and experience tell us that the personal risks to you as peace officers are greater than the risks you face on the street. Maybe it is time for us to devote at least as much attention to spiritual survival as we devote to street survival. Be careful out there…

Father,

Guide me always on the spiritual streets, so that I can survive not just in this life, but also in the life to come. Guide my family and friends, too. Help us exercise spiritual street-smarts and always avoid the devil's dangers, the culture's cons, and our own opposition to your will. Remind us to use the tools you give and the backup you provide. In the name of Christ, I pray,

Amen.

SHOOT OR DON'T SHOOT

THE STEADY DRIZZLE DEEPENED THE DARKNESS AND slowed my "Code Two" response, but the chill I felt didn't come from the cold night rain. It came from the call. Dispatch advised that the suspect was possibly armed with a handgun, possibly suicidal, and had earlier threatened to shoot his estranged wife and children. Even worse, he was now at the ranch trailer where his ex-wife lived; no further details except location and a general suspect description. I was en route with several other deputies and a backup Highway Patrol officer, but it was my call.

As we rolled up to the scene, I met two women at the trailer. One said that her husband had walked off with the suspect to calm him down and get him away from the others. She confirmed that the suspect had a gun. She said the other woman at the trailer was her sister, the suspect's ex-wife. Just then, I looked up the muddy road, and in the distance saw two men approaching on foot. "There they are," the woman said.

Not knowing the suspect's intent or capabilities, I wanted to stop him before he could close on the trailer. We had to move now. I asked the highway patrol officer to light up the two subjects and drive slowly toward them while we fanned out alongside his unit behind its lights. "No cover except the car," I thought. Couldn't be helped under the circumstances, but the darkness behind the lights of the advancing squad would afford us some concealment on our approach. If the suspect tried to shoot, he would have a hard time seeing us behind the blinding car lights. We, on the other hand, could catch him in a well-illuminated crossfire if the situation went sour. Our dispersal would also complicate his targeting problem and give him one more reason to keep things friendly.

> **I briefly wondered if the man thought he could take us on from behind the cover of his hostage or if maybe he was doing a suicide-by-cop routine. I would hate to have to oblige him.**

As we deployed and began our slow approach, I walked alongside the open door of the car. I asked the officer to use his loudspeaker to tell the two subjects to stop and put their hands out where we could see them. He jumped on the horn and gave the command, but we had a problem. The subjects didn't comply and kept walking toward us. More bad news, I suddenly realized. I couldn't identify the suspect because both subjects fit the description we had and I had not gotten a positive identification from the women at the trailer. To make things worse, I could only see three hands. One guy was walking in front of the other guy and I could see both of his empty hands. The subject walking behind him had his empty left hand visible, however, he was holding his right hand behind his back. My cop sense said he had a gun in that hand and the hair on the back of my neck agreed that this thing was going south in a hurry.

The circumstances gave weight to that feeling. The subject walking in front gave the appearance of a hostage screening a bad guy. The man in the rear seemed to be giving instructions to the man in the front. They kept ignoring our repeated commands to halt and the subject in the rear also ignored our shouts to show both hands. I briefly wondered if the man thought he could take us on from behind the cover of his hostage or if maybe he was doing a suicide-by-cop routine. I would hate to have to oblige him.

By now, all the deputies, myself included, had drawn down on the subject walking in the rear. As the men walked closer to our position, we got louder, yelling at them to stop and put their hands out where we could see them. They continued to ignore us and kept coming. The rear subject kept his right hand behind him, still out of sight.

They were about twenty feet away when the subject in the rear finally pulled his hand from behind his back and there it was—a huge .44 magnum Ruger Blackhawk, made bigger by my pucker factor. Single action, but even one shot was enough to ruin our whole day if the guy made a bad decision and was quick on the trigger. As he raised the gun in our direction, I could feel our preferred options ducking for cover. I began to squeeze my own trigger and knew my fellow officers were doing the same with their weapons.

Fortunately for the subject, our own guns were double-action, with a longer trigger pull and more pounds squeeze. This bought him one heartbeat. He bought three more by raising his gun slowly, depressing its muzzle slightly and leaving the hammer down. However, if he showed hostile intent by cocking the gun or twitching its business end up, even just a little, time would expire and so would he. Our decision was now riding on the edge of a very sharp razor.

We were taking a chance. We knew we probably couldn't react fast enough if the man with the gun chose to cap that first deadly round, but the same cop sense that earlier told me he was armed, now told me that he did not have that almost intangible, but all-important, hostile intent. As my blink-of-an-eye observation flashed its "Don't drop the hammer on this guy!" reaction to my trigger finger, one of the other deputies ran up from the subject's blind side and twisted the Ruger out of his hand. We grabbed both subjects, folded them over the hood of the highway patrol unit, cuffed and frisked them, until we could sort through who was who and what was what. Another dance with the devil was done.

"And now," as favorite radio legend Paul Harvey would say, "the rest of the story…" The suspect was not the one who had the gun. The suspect's brother-in-law had it. He had talked the suspect into giving him the gun and was simply walking back to give it to us. He had no coherent answer as to why he didn't comply with our commands. We were more than a little perturbed at him. And, I didn't feel sympathetic when he got a case of the shakes after realizing what a close shave it had been.

If we had shot the brother-in-law, we probably would have escaped criminal and maybe even civil liability for our mistake based on the circumstances. But, that would not have changed the shooting into anything less than a tragedy.

It couldn't have changed the fact that we would have shot a dense, but innocent citizen right in front of his wife. Harder to escape would have been the liability in our own hearts. We would have had to deal with a lifetime of guilt and the wife would have had to deal with a lifetime of loss. Fortunately, all the deputies, despite the risk to themselves, decided to hold fire. We made the correct decision, but we also knew how close it had been and it made a lasting impression on all of us. Years later, I can see and feel that scene as if it were yesterday.

Ours was a classic "shoot/ don't shoot" situation. We needed every ounce of our training, experience, attention, and judgment to make the right call. That is why police agencies spend much time, money and effort training their officers to deal with these scenarios. When I was at the FBI National Academy Associates annual conference a while back, I was amazed at the state-of-the-art equipment and training I saw on display. Why do agencies invest so much in "shoot/don't shoot?" The simple answer is that lethal force decisions are the most serious decisions in law enforcement. Society vests officers with a huge responsibility when it arms them and gives them the authority to make life and death choices. An officer's training, equipment, attitude, and actions need to equal this responsibility. Sometimes, despite an officer's best

> **The simple answer is that lethal force decisions are the most serious decisions in law enforcement.**

intentions, he or she can be involved in a "bad shoot," which tragically underscores the importance of proper preparation.

Is there a spiritual application in this story? Absolutely! Law enforcement is often a metaphor for life.

First, the knowledge and employment of sound spiritual principles is every bit as important as the knowledge and employment of sound tactical principles, sometimes more so, because of their eternal consequences.

> **Like law enforcement, life demands decisions, some of which are also life and death.**

Second, spiritual principles are as firm and immutable as tactical principles.

Third, like proper tactical principles, proper spiritual principles can, and must, be learned and applied.

Finally, like tactical principles, if we don't learn and apply spiritual principles, there WILL be tragic consequences. Peace officer statistics on suicide, divorce, alcoholism, etc. clearly confirm this sad truth. Conversely, believing and acting on sound spiritual principles is foundational to making the right call in life's difficult decisions.

Like law enforcement, life demands decisions, some of which are also life and death. And, as in "shoot/don't shoot" situations, if we blow the call, something or someone will tragically die. If we don't commit to having the best spiritual training, equipment, attitude and actions, we can kill hope, love, joy and peace in our lives. We can kill our physical or mental health, our marriages, our children, and even kill our relationship with God. To make the best shoot/don't shoot decisions of life, we need every possible ounce of sound spiritual backup. If we are deceived in belief and wrong in action, no amount of excuse-making will excuse us from the liability in our own hearts and lives.

The good news in all of this is that God understands and enables us to cope with the shoot/don't shoot situations of life. He is even there to back us up and pick up the pieces when we make a wrong call and have a spiritual "bad shoot," as we all have had.

Let me give you the two most important training tips I can think of to properly prepare you for your spiritual shoot/don't shoot situations of life. These come from the Bible, God's Word, our most important spiritual training manual:

1. "The fear of the Lord is the beginning of wisdom." Proverbs 1:7

   "The phrase, 'fear of the Lord' can be translated to mean that you hold a loving reverence for God that includes submission to his Lordship (or absolute sovereignty) and belief in His promises." ref. *Concordia Self-Study Bible*

2. "The work of God is this: to believe in the one He has sent." John 6:29

   "Believing (or trusting) in Jesus Christ is the indispensable 'work' God calls for, the one that leads to eternal life." ref. *Concordia Self-Study Bible*

God sent his Son into our critical incident world in response to our "officer down" spiritual situation. On his cross, God's Son willingly, in love, took the bullet of damnation that had our name on it. He rescued us from our hostage situation of eternal death and despair. Now, our most important shoot/don't shoot decision in life is to submit our lives in thanks and praise to the one who protects and serves us, our Ultimate Peace Officer, Jesus Christ.

This isn't a sermon, but a simple truth. This is life. Typically, officers, even good officers, tend to neglect their spiritual shoot/don't shoot training. This is easy to do because the consequences of spiritual neglect are often hidden from us until it is too late.

> **Do you believe God's truth, trust God's love and obey God's protective commands?**

So, now it's time for a gut check. Where are you in your spiritual "shoot/don't shoot" preparation? Have you adopted our two training tips? Is God's Word an integral part of your life? Do you have the backup of other believers, especially through the fellowship of a good church? How often do you talk to God in prayer? Do you believe God's truth, trust God's love and obey God's protective commands? It's all about "shoot or don't shoot."

Lord,

Sometimes in this world we ride a fine, feathered edge between a lot of things that can make or break us in life: smart or dumb, hope or despair, confidence or arrogance, love or hate, victory or defeat, honor or shame, and life or death. Help me make the right call at the right moment, Lord. Keep me from going over the edge in the wrong direction. Forgive me for the times I've failed (confess here those things that have burdened you with guilt, understanding that God's purpose is not to convict you, but to comfort and forgive you). Forgive me for the times I've doubted (admit here your struggles and ask for his help with each one specifically). Thank you that, because of Jesus, you do forgive and forget. Help me to forgive and forget too, so I can have your peace and joy,

Amen.

VERSES TO USE IN
ARRESTING...

THE BIBLE IS NOT JUST A COLLECTION OF OLD LETTERS written by dead people. It is not a book of "feel good" advice. It is the living and active "Sword of the Spirit."

Hebrews 4:12 says, "God's Word is living and active. It is sharper than any two-edged sword and cuts as deep as the place where soul and spirit meet, the place where joints and marrow meet. God's word judges a person's thoughts and intentions." Because we can't hide from God, everything we do is uncovered and exposed for Him to see. As a result, we answer to Him.

The Bible gives us the spiritual authority for the choices we make in work and in life.

The Bible gives us the spiritual authority for the choices we make in work and in life. It provides our power, training, tools and backup to confront evil as Christ's "peace officers." Good peace officers know their business, stay alert and aggressive, and maintain and properly use the tools of their trade. Christ's

Stephen C. Lee

peace officers do the same. We need to properly and aggressively wield the Word, the sword of the Spirit, in our spiritual battles.

On the following pages, you will find a wide variety of Bible verses to use in some of life's most difficult moments. My encouragement to you is to keep a bookmark here and be ready to read these verses at a moment's notice. Additionally, you might want to take the time to memorize the verses that especially speak to you. It will be an investment of your time and energy to do so, but you will be amazed how quickly those verses come to your mind at exactly the right time. Finally, work on compiling your own list of backup passages to give you guidance and strength in confronting life's challenges.

Verses To Use in Arresting . . .

ABUSE
Matthew 18:21-35; 1 Corinthians 13; Ephesians 5:21-6:4; Colossians 3:19-21; 2 Timothy 3; 1 John 3; 1 Peter 3:7

ADDICTION
Proverbs 25:28; John 8:32, 36; Romans 6:12-14, 12:1-2; Galatians 5:16-26; Ephesians 5:18

ADULTERY
Genesis 2:24, 39:2-12; Leviticus 18:20; Exodus 20:14; Proverbs 5, 6:24-29; Matthew 5:27-30

ANGER
Proverbs 14:29; 15:1, 29:11; Matthew 5:21-26; Ephesians 4:26-32; James 1:19-20; Galatians 5:20

ANGUISH
Psalm 118:5; Lamentations 3

ANXIETY
Psalm 94:19, 139; Proverbs 12:25; John 14:27;
Philippians 4:6; 1 Peter 5:7

ARGUMENTS
Psalm 133; Proverbs 15:18; Philippians 2:14;
2 Timothy 2:23; Titus 3:9

ARROGANCE
Psalm 119:78; Romans 1-3; 1 Timothy 6:17; James 4:6;
Proverbs 6:17

BETRAYAL
Genesis 37:17-20; 45:1-15; Psalm 41; Luke 22:47, 23:32-34;
Acts 2:22-39; Romans 8:28

BITTERNESS
Luke 23:34; Romans 8:28; Ephesians 4:31; Colossians 3:13;
Hebrews 12:15

BOASTING
Galatians 6:14; James 4:13-16; 1 Corinthians 13:4;
2 Corinthians 10:17

BRIBERY & EXTORTION
Exodus 23:8; Psalm 26; 62; Proverbs 11:18, 15:27;
Ecclesiastes 7:7; Luke 3:14

BROKEN HEARTEDNESS
Psalm 34:18; 147:3; Isaiah 61:1; Luke 4:14-21; Matthew 5:4

COMPLACENCY
Psalm 90; Proverbs 1:20-33; Matthew 24:42-44;
Hebrews 7:7-12; Luke 12:15-21; 2 Peter 3

CONCEIT
Romans 12:3, 12:16; Galatians 5:25-26; Philippians 2:3-11;
James 4:10

CORRUPTION
Psalm 1, 17, 53; Proverbs 4:24-27, 22:24-25, 24:1-2;
1 Corinthians 15:33-34

COARSE TALK
Exodus 20:7; Matthew 5:33-37; Ephesians 4:29-32, 5:4;
James 3:2-12

DARKNESS
Psalm 18:28, 139:12; Isaiah 42:16; Matthew 4:12-17;
John 8:12; Romans 13:12; 1 Peter 2:9; 1 John 1:5

DEATH
Psalm 23; Romans 8:11, 8:31-39; 1 Corinthians 15: 12-58;
John 3:16; 1 Thessalonians 1:3-18

DECEPTION
Jeremiah 17:9; John 8:32; Ephesians 4:14-15, 25

DEFEAT &ADVERSITY
Romans 5:3-5, 7:14-25; Hebrews 2:17-18;
1 Thessalonians 1:2-10; James 1:2-4

DEPRESSION
Psalm 42, 43, 55, 62, 77, 88, 102, 103, 116, 138:7

DESPAIR
Psalm 22, 27:13-14, 43:5; 2 Corinthians 4:7-18

DEVIL
Matthew 4:1-11; 2 Corinthians 11:4; 2 Thessalonians 2;
James 4:7; 1 Peter 5:8; Revelation 20:10

DISASTER
Psalm 46, 57:1, 91; Proverbs 3:25-26

DISCONTENT
Philippians 4:10-13, 4:19; 1 Timothy 6:6-8; Hebrews 13:5;
Matthew 6:33

DISCOURAGEMENT
Romans 15:4; Philippians 1:6; 1 Thessalonians 5:16-18

DISRESPECT
Exodus 20:12; Romans 13:1-7; 1 Timothy 5:1;
2 Timothy 2:1-2, 3:2; 1 Peter 2:13-17, 5:5

DISSIPATION & DRUNKENNESS
Proverbs 20:1; 23:20-35; Luke 21:34; Romans 13:13-14;
Titus 2:11-13; 1 Peter 4:3; Ephesians 5:18

DIVORCE
Proverbs 5:15-20, 31; Malachi 2:13-16;
Matthew 5:32-32, 19:1-9

DOUBT
Psalm 145; Proverbs 3:5-6; Mark 9:24; John 20:24-31;
Romans 10:9-15, 15:13; James 1:6

ENEMIES
Psalm 59,61,64; Proverbs 16:7; Matthew 5:44;
Luke 6:27-36; Romans 5:6-11

ERROR
Proverbs 14:12; 2 Timothy 3:14-17; James 5:19-20;
1 John 4:1-6

EVIL
Psalm 1, 7:9, 34:11-17; Matthew 6:13; Romans 12:9

EXPLOITATION
Proverbs 3:29, 22:22-23, 28: 8, 24

EXTREMISM
Proverbs 6:16-19; Ecclesiastes 7:18; 2 Corinthians 12:20;
Galatians 5:19-21

FALSEHOOD
Exodus 23:6-7; Proverbs 13:5; 19:5; Luke 3:14; John 8:42-47

FAULT, FAULTFINDING
Psalm 19:12-14; Matthew 7:1-5, 18:15-35; John 8:7

FAVORITISM
Leviticus 19:15; Acts 10:34; 1 Timothy 5:21; James 2: 1-13

FEAR
Psalm 23; 27; 121; Proverbs 1:7; Isaiah 51:7-8;
Matthew 10:28; 1 John 4:16-18

FLATTERY
Psalm 12; Proverbs 11:13, 16:28, 26:28;
1 Thessalonians 2:3-6

FOOLISHNESS
Proverbs 14:15-18, 26:1-12; 1 Corinthians 1:18-31;
Ephesians 5:1-21

GOSSIP
Psalm 101, 140; Proverbs 11:13, 26:20-28; James 3:2-6

GREED
Matthew 6:19-24; Luke 12:15; Colossians 3:5;
1 Timothy 6:9-19; Hebrews 13:5

GUILT
Psalm 32, 51, 130, 143; 2 Corinthians 7:10; 1 John 1:9;
Romans 8:1

HATRED
Proverbs 25:21-22; 1 Corinthians 13; Galatians 5:13-15;
1 John 4:7-21

HOPELESSNESS
Psalm 43:5; Romans 5:5, 15:4, 13, 43:5

HYPOCRISY
Proverbs 10:9; Matthew 7:1-5; 23; 1 Peter 2:1-3

IDOLATRY
Exodus 20:1-6; 1 Samuel 15:16-23; 1 Corinthians 10:14;
Ephesians 5:5

IMMORALITY
Matthew 15:1-20; Romans 13:8-14; 1 Corinthians 6:12-20

IMPURITY & INTEMPERANCE
Mark 7:1-23; Ephesians 5:1-20; Colossians 3:17

INACTION
Proverbs 3:5-6; Romans 12:1-2; James 2:14-26;
1 Peter 1:13-25

INEQUALITY
John 3:16; Acts 10:34; Romans 2:11; Galatians 3:26-28;
Ephesians 6:9

INJUSTICE
Deuteronomy 15:19-20; Psalm 69, 82, 94, 146;
Proverbs 14:31

INSULTS
Proverbs 12:16; Matthew 5:11; 1 Peter 3:9;
2 Peter 2:21-23, 3:9

JEALOUSY & ENVY
Exodus 20:17; Proverbs 14:30; James 3:13-18;
Galatians 5:19-21

LAZINESS
Proverbs 6:6-11, 10:4, 19:24, 26:13-165; Hebrews 6:10-12;
2 Thessalonians 3:10

LIES
Exodus 20:16; 23:1-3; Leviticus 19:11; Psalm 27:12;
Proverbs 19:28, 26:18-19

LONELINESS
1 Kings 19; Psalm 25:16, 32, 34, 68:4-10;
John 14:16-20, 14: 25-27

LUST
Romans 1:21-27; 1 Thessalonians 4:3-8; 1 Peter 4:15-16;
1 John 2:15-17

PAIN, INJURY & SICKNESS
Psalm 103; 2 Corinthians 4:7-18, 12:7-10; James 5:13-18;
Revelation 21:4

PERJURY
Malachi 3:5; Proverbs 6:17, 24:28, Luke 3:14;
1 Timothy 1:8-11

PERSECUTION
Psalm 32, 35, 118, 142; 2 Timothy 3:1-13; 1 Peter 4:12-19

POWERLESSNESS
Psalm 147:5; Proverbs 24:5; 2 Corinthians 12:9; James 5:16

PRIDE
Psalm 10; Proverbs 16:25; Romans 12:16;
1 Corinthians 10:1-12; James 4:6

REBELLION
1 Samuel 15:23; Proverbs 17:11, 29:1, 1 Timothy 1:9

RECKLESSNESS
Proverbs 12:18, 14:16; Matthew 12:36

REVENGE
Deuteronomy 32:34-43; Matthew 5:38-48;
Romans 12:17-21; 1 Peter 3:9

SELFISHNESS
1 Corinthians 10:24; Philippians 2:1-22; James 3:13-18;
1 Peter 5:2-4

SHAME
Psalm 25, 34:5; Proverbs 13:18; Joel 2:25-27;
2 Corinthians 4:2

SIN
Romans 6:23, 8:1-17; Galatians 5:16-6:9;
Hebrews 12:1-4; James 1:13-15

SORCERY & WITCHCRAFT
Exodus 22:18; Leviticus 19:26-31; Revelation 21:8

SORROW
Psalm 6, 23, 30, 116, 126; Isaiah 60:19-20;
Revelation 21:1-5

SUFFERING
Romans 5:3-5, 8:17-39; 1 Corinthians 12:26;
Philippians 3:7-21

TEMPTATION
1 Corinthians 10:13; 2 Timothy 2:22; Hebrews 4:14-16;
1 Peter 5:8-11

TIMIDITY
Romans 3:23, 34:5;1 Thessalonians 5:14-15; 2 Timothy 1:7

TRAGEDY & SORROW
Romans 8:18-39; 2 Corinthians 1:3-7;
1 Thessalonians 4:13-18

TROUBLE
Psalm 9:9, 32:7, 46:1, 50:15, 59:16; Proverbs 11:17;
John 14:1, 16:33

UNBELIEF
Psalm 14:1, 19, 95, 100, 127:1; Romans 1:18-22;
1 Timothy 1

WEARINESS
Isaiah 40:28-31; Matthew 11:28-30; Galatians 6:9

WICKEDNESS
Psalm 1, 10, 73; Proverbs 4; Romans 1; 1 Corinthians 6:9-11

WORLDLINESS
Mark 8:36; Romans 12:1-2; 1 John 2:15-17, 5:19

WORRY
Psalm 56:3; Matthew 6:25-34; Philippians 4:6-7;
1 Peter 5:6-7

"JOHN WAYNE" SYNDROME

In Officer Survival Training, it's called "John Wayne Syndrome." As an example, officer "John Wayne" pulls over a traffic violator and doesn't call in the car stop. Maybe his radio is busy and he doesn't want to wait for a break in traffic, or maybe he just doesn't want to take the trouble to deal with dispatch. Instead, he swaggers up to the stopped vehicle, sure in his own mind that this potentially dangerous law enforcement task is "just routine." He has made such stops hundreds of times before without a problem. Why should this one be any different? So, his approach is careless. He doesn't watch the driver's hands. He ignores the passengers. When the occupants of the vehicle begin to act suspiciously, he doesn't call for help, for backup. Instead, he handles an escalating problem by himself, and so, he winds up dead—a victim of John Wayne Syndrome.

> **He handles an escalating problem by himself, and so, he winds up dead— a victim of John Wayne Syndrome.**

An officer with this syndrome may be a hero in his own

mind, but, in reality, his I-walk-on-water attitude is a foolish and deadly kind of heroism. Good officer survival instructors teach that independence and arrogance will get you killed. They emphasize that officers should not play with John Wayne, but should ask for backup. This is not being weak. It's being street-smart.

Some time ago, I attended an FBI LEOKA (Law Enforcement Officers Killed and Assaulted) Seminar. I was impressed by the attention given to street survival issues, but, at the same time, I couldn't help remembering that there are other, more snake-subtle threats. For example, peace officers are eight times more likely to commit suicide than to be murdered in the line of duty. This shocking statistic highlights a tragic irony. As peace officers, we devote a great deal of training to street survival, but too often fail to address other office survival issues, such as suicide. These other threats may be less obvious and immediate, but they are no less deadly. The grim reality is that an officer faces more threats from within than from without, but typically spends more time preparing for threats from without than from within. The more that we understand and act on this fact, the less we'll adopt a John Wayne attitude toward personal survival issues.

> **As peace officers, we devote a great deal of training to street survival, but too often fail to address other office survival issues, such as suicide.**

Craig W. took a John Wayne Syndrome type of approach to his personal life. He was a respected street-smart F.T.O (Field Training Officer), with a good personality and a great sense of humor. He helped train me as an officer and I was impressed by him and his abilities. What I and others didn't know was that he had some personal struggles that were compounded by a drinking problem. One night, we got a call to Craig's house. He had a revolver, plenty of ammunition and he was drunk. He held us off with gunfire for several hours. Fortunately, no one was hurt, but obviously, Craig had a career-ender that night. I tried talking to him after the incident, but "John Wayne Craig" refused to deal with his problems. He moved to another state and later died in an accident.

Craig is an extreme example, but many other officers do not pay sufficient attention to emotional or relational survival. As a consequence, their marriages, their families and their lives fall apart. More fundamentally, many officers pay *no* attention to spiritual survival. They have no spiritual foundation and, consequently, are vulnerable to all the storms of life. I've labeled this vulnerability as, "threat neglect."

> ## "What good will it do for people to win the whole world and lose their lives?"

Do you neglect threats? If you are a peace officer, there are many reasons you may do so. For example, the psychologist, Abraham Maslow, spoke about a "hierarchy of needs." He said that physical needs, including the need for physical safety and security, have to be satisfied before other and less tangible needs can be addressed. Maslow's theory may help explain why some officers have trouble moving beyond physical survival issues to examine their relationship and emotional issues. However, although other survival issues may be less pressing than immediate physical ones, they are no less important.

Jesus points out that spiritual survival is the most important kind of survival. He said that, "man does not live on bread alone, but on every word that comes from the mouth of God," (Matthew 4:4). This spiritual truth has very practical applications. For instance, if an officer is tempted to "eat" his or her gun, physical survival may very well depend on spiritual health.

I had a good talk with a state trooper during a ride-along a while back. We applied the John Wayne Syndrome principle to the spiritual side of life. He and I agreed that officers—for a variety of reasons—typically have a very hard time asking for and receiving help in their personal lives. Like John Wayne, they try to gut it out on their own rather than call for spiritual backup and, as a consequence, a variety of "bad guys," including suicide, divorce, breakdown, cynicism, despair, etc., claim them.

Jesus says in Matthew 16:26, "What good will it do for people to win the whole world and lose their lives? Or what will a person give in exchange for life?" Applied to officer spiritual survival, this statement could read, "What good will it be for an officer to survive on the street, yet the rest of his life goes down the tubes?"

I love old John Wayne movies, but the Word of God and experience have taught me not to confuse life with the movies. Both street survival and spiritual survival depend on abandoning John Wayne Syndrome and asking for help when we need it. (By the way, I heard that, at the end of his life, John Wayne became a Christian. Maybe it's just a rumor…)

What kind of spiritual "routine traffic stop" are you on today? Are you prepared? Have you adopted the best attitude and actions, or are you playing a make-believe John Wayne in the face of for-real survival threats? Street-smart officers learn and practice good officer survival skills.

I invite you to extend this learning and practice to every area of your life. And, remember that Christ is "in service" and waiting to be your backup.

Father,

It's tough to admit I need help sometimes, especially since I've been conditioned in my profession to always carry an attitude of control and a demeanor of "command presence." However, life in general is like the street in particular. If I'm not careful, that attitude and that demeanor, carried too far with "John Wayne" actions, can get me dead in a hurry. Sometimes the smart thing to do is simply call for backup, so that's what I want to do right now…(here tell God what you need help with in your life). Help me to always be aware of when I need help and wise enough to ask for it—from you or anyone else who can help,

Amen.

"The Lord supports everyone who falls. He straightens the backs of those who are bent over. The eyes of all creatures look to you, and you give them their food at the proper time. You open your hand, and you satisfy the desire of every living thing. The Lord is fair in all his ways and faithful in everything he does. The Lord is near to everyone who prays to him, to every faithful person who prays to him. He fills the needs of those who fear him. He hears their cries for help and saves them." *Psalm 145:14-19*

"If you declare that Jesus is Lord, and believe that God brought him back to life, you will be saved. By believing you receive God's approval, and by declaring your faith you are saved. Scripture says, "Whoever believes in him will not be ashamed." There is no difference between Jews and Greeks. They all have the same Lord, who gives his riches to everyone who prays to him." *Romans 10:9-13*

THE COP AT THE CROSS

CORNELIUS NOTED THE TREMOR IN HIS HAND AS HE reached for the wine and cursed himself again. This was no way for a soldier to react, especially a centurion of Pilate's Praetorium. But, after two sleepless nights, since the crucifixion of that man, he didn't really care. Besides, he thought grimly, except for the gate guard, I'm the only one awake this early on Sunday morning. Who would be fool enough to disturb a Roman officer in his barracks atop Jerusalem's Antonia Fortress? No, there would be no witnesses to his shame. No witnesses to his fear, guilt and self-doubt. No witnesses, none but the eyes of that man on the cross.

"I wish he would let me live in peace," Cornelius muttered. He spoke of the man from Nazareth in the present tense, although he knew that man was dead. He had seen with his own eyes the dark post-mortem blood flowing from the spear-pierced side. But, how could you finally and forever kill a man like that? Somehow, at the foot of Jesus' cross, Cornelius had discovered the true answer to that question. In the past two days that truth had turned his self-ordered world upside down. He could not sleep. He could not think.

In the early morning darkness, he ducked those eyes and raised his cup in mock salute, "A tribute to Mark Antony,

whose walls here protect me from all but my own thoughts."
He then bowed an exaggerated bow. "Homage also to my
ancestor, Cornelius Sulla, whose nerve has failed his name-
sake. He freed 10,000 slaves from their bondage, but that
dead hero is powerless to free this one tortured captive from
the tyranny of his own dark dreams!" Angrily he drew his
sword and shouted, "Sic Semper Tyrannis! Thus Always to
Tyrants!" Then the fear washed over him again. Cornelius
retreated, slumping in his chair. He stared down at his blood-
red reflection in the cup. His dark, dead eyes stared back and
he softly quoted, "The eyes are the window of the soul…"

He first saw a reflection of
that other man's eyes in the eyes
of his compatriot from Capernaum. Several months ago he
had met that God-fearing centurion in Caesarea at the garri-
son of the Italian Regiment.
What was his name? The story
was ridiculous at first. The centurion claimed to have a servant
who was miraculously healed by
a man called "Jesus," of the city
of Nazareth. He was radiant
about that healer, which was no way for a professional soldier
to behave. But the eyes of his centurion friend spoke truth. As
a Roman officer who routinely interrogated suspects,
Cornelius had learned through hard experience that "lips con-
ceal—eyes reveal." The eyes of the centurion from Capernaum corroborated his lips. Mirrored in that soldier's eyes

> **Mirrored in that soldier's eyes were the eyes of Jesus, and in that reflection, the ridiculous was transformed into reality.**

were the eyes of Jesus, and in that reflection, the ridiculous was transformed into reality.

Cornelius put that encounter out of his mind. It did not fit into the concrete world he had shaped according to Rome's rules and his own passions. But then, that divine man re-entered his world. Early last Friday Cornelius was on duty in the Praetorium when the Jewish leaders showed up with a prisoner for Pilate, the beaten and bloody Jesus of Nazareth. Cornelius had noticed the man's eyes immediately. Such a contrast to his disheveled and disfigured appearance! True, there was pain in those eyes. And, there was a deep and nameless sorrow. But in those divine eyes there was no fear, or anger, or hatred or even despair. Instead, there shone through from the man's soul an infinite goodness. Infinite peace. Infinite strength. Infinite wisdom. Infinite authority. Infinite life. And, an infinite unknown. What was it?

And Jesus looked with those God-filled eyes toward the skies, as if he knew beyond certainty itself that his heavenly Father would reclaim his condemned Son.

Because of the discipline befitting a solider, despite his growing doubt, Cornelius had issued the orders from Pontius Pilate, "Take him! Strip him! Beat him!...Crucify him!" Cornelius shuddered in his soul. What a mockery of justice for Pilate to release that other known criminal, Barabbas, instead of Jesus! What cowardice before the crowd! But,

Cornelius knew he was no better. He had hidden his own fear and guilt behind a façade of duty. He had hidden behind Pilate's orders.

That divine man. He suffered as a man, but not like a man. Cornelius' soldiers had mocked the man from Nazareth for his apparent pretensions, "King?" "Son of God?" "We'll show you!" "Let's cover your eyes and see if you can tell us who hit you! We'll lay open your back with a whip, right down to the bone. Let's see if the Son of God bleeds!" And, "Where is your Father, if he is God?" The mocking words of his soldiers now haunted Cornelius with their unintended truth. That truth mocked him for his own cowardice and evil.

"My God, my God, why have you forsaken me?" The words of Jesus on the cross seemed to confirm the soldiers' taunts. But, then Cornelius heard Jesus continue more quietly, as if quoting from a sacred passage.* And Jesus looked with those God-filled eyes toward the skies, as if he knew beyond certainty itself that his heavenly Father would reclaim his condemned Son.

The Son of God? Cornelius was not accustomed to think of just one all-supreme God. The thought frightened him. A human could in some way divide and conquer a petty pantheon of corrupt Roman gods, but one righteous God who ruled all? Such a God would tolerate no competition or contradiction. And to have God's righteous Son on earth, only to be crucified by the very creatures he had created? How great must be his anger, especially for the centurion who had supervised the execution! In the flickering light of the lamp, Cornelius looked at his hands, the hands that had tortured so many, and now had killed the Son of God himself. Those hands were the instruments of his own hard and hopeless heart. Pilate had washed his hands with water, but his guilt remained. Cornelius had washed his heart with wine, but his guilt also remained. In despair, he threw his cup against the wall and buried his head in his blood-guilty hands.

He had watched him die on that cross. It was actually a process of slow suffocation, as the exhausted Jesus could no longer push himself up to draw breath. But he had not suffocated to death. Instead, it was as if he had allowed himself to die. Cornelius remembered his cry, "It is finished!" But, it was not the cry of a man dying in despair. It was the cry of a man who had completely committed himself to a monumental task and had now victoriously done it. Cornelius recognized that cry. It was the cry of a conquering soldier.

More than the terrifying miracles of that darkened sky and earthquake at the cross, it was the memory of Jesus' eyes that had kept Cornelius awake for two nights. He could still see the eternity in those eyes…along with that infinite something else. What could it be?

"Father, forgive them, for they know not what they do." Softly, the words of Jesus came back to Cornelius. Softly, like the coming dawn, they lightened the gloom in his heart. He had never heard words like those before. They bore the same authority as those miracles that had cowered him at the cross, but now that authority brought comfort instead of fear. Cornelius recognized authority. In Jesus' words of forgiveness, he heard the authority of God himself proclaiming Cornelius' own pardon. Like the lamp in his room, a flame began to flicker in his dark, dead heart, fed by the powerful words of

Jesus, "Father forgive them, for they know not what they do."

Suddenly, in the breaking day, he heard soldiers, his soldiers, crashing through the doors of the Praetorium below. Cornelius shook himself from his reverie and ran out the door and down to the courtyard. There he recovered his command presence and confronted the milling mob. "What's going on here?" he demanded. One of the men stepped forward, out of breath. "The tomb, sir. The one Pilate ordered us to watch. They must have stolen his body while we were sleeping. That man we crucified on Friday—Jesus of Nazareth. They took him, sir." Cornelius looked into the soldiers' eyes and there found what he knew he would find, fear and deception. "You lie," he said simply. He pushed through the soldiers and started to run.

This tomb...it smelled like Spring.

The large, round stone lay by the side of the tomb, it's broken seal silently mocking not just Pilate, but death itself. He stepped up to the entrance and slowly peered inside. Empty. A carved rock bier in the far wall. Empty. Grave clothes neatly folded on top of the bier. Empty. A faint aroma of myrrh and aloes. Something besides the body was missing. What was it? Cornelius had been at many death scenes before, but this was different. Then it came to him. The smell was missing, that unforgettable sick sweet death smell that clung to nostrils and hair and clothes and tombs and made a person want to retch and bathe. Cornelius stepped inside and sniffed in surprise. This tomb...it smelled like Spring.

At that moment, he again saw that man's eyes with their

infinite unknown...Cornelius realized that his very life depended on understanding that mystery. He leaned against the wall of the empty tomb and tightly closed his eyes. He felt again that man's presence and, for the first time in his life, tears flowed down his face. Tears of sorrow and pain. Tears of guilt and shame. Tears for a lost innocence that he did not even remember. Tears of longing. Then, in that longing, in that moment, he saw his tears reflected in the tear-stained face of Jesus and he knew. The man on the cross had not cried for *himself*. The man on the cross had cried for *Cornelius*. The man on the cross had died for *him*. What Pilate's water could never do, what Cornelius' wine could never do, Jesus' blood had done. Only blood could atone for blood. Only divine blood could redeem the blood of the entire world.

At last, Cornelius understood Jesus' soldier sacrifice. Jesus, the mortal man, had fallen on the sword of sin for all of us. Jesus, the immortal Son of God, had washed away all our sin with his blood. In that God-empowered moment, Cornelius was forever changed.

From pain to peace.
From guilt to grace.
From fear to faith.
From sorrow to salvation.
From tragedy to triumph.
From the lost to the living.

*Read Psalm 22, prophetically written 1,000 years before Christ's crucifixion.

He finally and forever saw that infinite unknown, unknown no more, in the eyes of the God/man, Jesus. It was love. Eyes still closed to the world, but now opened to eternity, he beheld the love of God and, there in the empty tomb, Cornelius the Christian bowed before his living Savior and King.

May the sure and certain Easter hope of Jesus Christ be yours!

Jesus,
Thank you for opening my eyes to the love in yours,
Amen.

"The Lord has not despised or been disgusted with the plight of the oppressed one. He has not hidden his face from that person. The Lord heard when that oppressed person cried out to him for help." *Psalm 22:24*

HELP!
I'M MARRIED TO A COP!

ACCORDING TO STATISTICS, AND VERIFIED BY OUR experience, the divorce rate for peace officers is above 80%. Staggering, isn't it? This sad fact compels me to write some thoughts about marriage in general, and law enforcement marriages in particular.

Before I even tackle the subject of what makes a great marriage, let me say that I understand many, many of you feel a sense of pain and loss because of divorce in your lives. This may resurrect emotionally-charged memories of that book you bought, the audiotape you listened to, that seminar you attended and that counseling you received, all in the vain hope of reviving a dead or dying marriage. So, I continue with these thoughts knowing that, for some of you, healing continues from a past relationship, while you look with hope to the future. My intent here is not

> **The relationship itself is larger than either individual and they each defer to that truth.**

to beat up on wounded people, but to prevent others from being wounded.

A few years ago, I attended a seminar hosted by the Colorado Law Enforcement Officers Association. Dr. John Nicoletti, PH.D., and Ms. Lottie Flater, LCSW, of Nicoletti-Flater Associates, spoke in a session titled, "Law Enforcement Occupation and High Risk Relationships." The title reflects the obvious truth that law enforcement poses risks to relationships.

In pointing out the key element in making a marriage work, Dr. Nicoletti, a police psychologist, stated that research shows that the common denominator of *all* successful marriages is this foundational belief: "Survival of the marriage relationship is more important than the individual ego." This simply

> **I am convinced of one overriding truth—that our society's heavy emphasis on self-fulfillment and the rights of the individual have played havoc with marriages today.**

means that the marriage as a whole is greater than the marriage parts. The relationship itself is larger than either individual and they each defer to that truth. There is a simple refusal to resort to divorce. A commitment is made by a man and a woman to stick it out, "come hell or high water."

If two people have this commitment, it ultimately does not matter if they read the books, listen to the tapes, attend the seminar or receive counseling. They will remain married simply because their marriage together is more important to them than is their individual lives alone. Conversely, if two people do not have this commitment, it ultimately does not matter if they devote themselves to all the methods of marriage improvement, because they will divorce. It's that obvious. It's that simple. However, it's also that hard.

> **"What greater love is there than to endure despite hardship, sickness and failure?"**

When I listen to an officer say to me, "Chaplain Steve, you don't understand my situation…" I already know that, as a result of this attitude, he or she has planted the seeds of divorce. This common attitude is one reason why Dr. Nicolletti stated that we are living in an age of "serial marriage." Many officers today have given up on the traditional belief that marriage can and should last a lifetime, as they drift from one relationship to another. They give up on each marriage in turn, as, in the words of a country Western song, "the tingle becomes a chill."

I am convinced of one overriding truth—that our society's heavy emphasis on self-fulfillment and the rights of the individual have played havoc with marriages today. The fundamental requirement for a successful marriage is the willingness of two people to sacrifice their rights and place the needs of the marriage ahead of the needs of the individual. Many are no longer willing to make that sacrifice. Ironically, because of that self-centered perspective, many people in our society are unable to find self-fulfillment, because true self-fulfillment comes from meeting the needs of another.

Stop for a moment and consider the traditional wedding vows which state, "For better, for worse, for richer, for poorer, in sickness and in health, to love and to cherish, until death parts us." If you examine each of these elements of marriage you will quickly see that marriage holds trying times, negative times, disappointing times and uncomfortable times. These unpleasant realities of every marriage will sink the ship if there is no abiding commitment to save it from the storms.

Some may ask, "But, what about the legacy of misery that has been passed on from marriages that have been loveless, but have endured, for the sake of the children or for some other less-noble-than-love practical reason? Let me ask this in reply, "How noble is it to undergo a series of broken relationships that traumatize children with change, devastate finances, create emotional, spiritual and even physical problems and generally set individuals and families adrift on a sea of instability?" Let me also ask, "What greater love is there than to endure despite hardship, sickness and failure?"

> **It takes a solid commitment foundation to build a great marriage home.**

Here some of you may ask, "What am I supposed to do if I'm divorced as a result of circumstances beyond my control, despite all my efforts to sustain my marriage?" If you're divorced, you already know the high cost of the process, and I'm not just talking dollars here. All of those issues with children, friendships, day-to-day living, and the rest of the divorce package can bring you to your knees.

And, that's a good thing. Stay on your knees as you take the hand that you've been dealt and give that hand right back to God. The Bible tells us that nothing separates us from his love. People may fail us and circumstances may force changes to our lives that were never intended or expected. But, he is not ever going to give up on his commitment to you. He will keep you going on those days when you feel isolated or depressed by your circumstances.

Marriage is a home for two people. For peace officers, it is a haven from the streets and the ugly realities we sometimes must face in the line of duty. Just like a good house, it must have a firm foundation. That foundation is the commitment by each spouse to put the survival of the marriage *first* on the list of personal priorities, come what may.

You may be thinking, "Steve, what you are describing sounds more like a life sentence in a prison. I don't want to just survive a marriage. I want to have a great marriage." We'll address this further, but for now, here's the point: It takes a solid commitment foundation to build a great marriage home. Otherwise, the greatest marriage structure will wash away in the unavoidable storms of life.

Some time ago, I chaired a skills competition among law enforcement students at a local community college. After the mandatory part of the program, I offered an optional workshop for the students on "Officer Survival—Dealing with the Other Risks." Here I addressed the reality that the most dangerous threats to a peace officer are not physical, but are emotional, relational, and spiritual. One student asked me for the most important factor in a successful marriage. I replied that the choice of a partner was the most important factor. I went on to explain that I was not talking about compatibility, but commitment. It is most important to choose a partner who will be committed to the marriage for a lifetime (obviously both should have this same commitment). With that commitment by both partners, a marriage will survive.

It is important to take time to carefully establish a person's commitment *before* the marriage. Do not turn a blind eye, as so many do, to "suspicious circumstances" that indicate a person's lack of commitment. You will pay a terrible price if you do. Take the time to let your relationship grow deeply before jumping into marriage. Observe how your potential mate conducts his or her relationship with God, friends and family. A potential partner, eager to "seal the deal," can easily claim to be committed to marriage, but his or her actions and relationships with others will tell you whether or not that person is one who will solidly make that lifetime commitment.

The truth is, the solid commitment that sustains a marriage doesn't just happen. It doesn't simply come from an inner determination to "get the job done right." The resolve, the drive to survive, comes from two people who stand before God in making their vows; who support each other before God in keeping those vows; and who keep a close eye on the wily ways of the devil every step of the way. That commitment, to God and each other as a whole, is exactly what gets you through the long haul—even when the "getting" is hard, painful, frustrating and downright exhausting.

Now, about that "great marriage." If two people have committed unalterably to a lifetime together, that reality will be a great motivator to work out problems rather than to "bail out." Here is the appropriate place to be aggressively proactive. This is the time to read the books, listen to the tapes, attend the seminars, take the tests and get the counseling. People exist in a physical, emotional, relational and spiritual world. To have a great marriage, a couple must address each of these areas in their life together. To neglect any of these areas poses dangerous risks. For instance, if a partner suffers from depression, it may be necessary to see a doctor and get a prescription for an anti-depressant. This one action step can make all the difference in the world. As another example, a couple that, "prays together, stays together." Prayer holds remarkable power! And, don't forget *regular* church attendance. There are dozens of ways for a couple to improve their marriage. If you don't know what they are, commit to finding them.

> **A couple needs to commit to a physical, emotional, relational and spiritual intimacy that is unique and not shared with any other human being.**

Part of commitment is establishing boundaries of protection around marriage. A couple needs to commit to a physical, emotional, relational and spiritual intimacy that is unique and not shared with any other human being. To do otherwise is to invite adultery and divorce. I know too many officers who have been unwilling to place boundaries around a good marriage and have paid a terrible price for their thick-headedness. You must be willing. Don't wait until it is too late.

My wife has survived 24 years of marriage to me. We have successfully come through a law enforcement career and a change to full-time ministry. We have what I consider to be a great marriage and we have four wonderful children. We have also had to deal with significant problems. We still have ups and downs and I imagine we always will. The one saving grace in our marriage has been exactly that—saving grace. We forgive and accept each other, just as God forgives and accepts us. I dearly love my wife and she dearly loves me, not because we are perfect, but because we have each provided a secure home for the other where we are loved *no matter what*. Believe me, our marriage is worth the commitment. Yours is, too!

Great marriages don't just happen. They take commitment. To have that successful relationship, begin now with a commitment to Jesus Christ, who committed his life to you. He will enable both you and your spouse to live out your marriage vows by the power of His Holy Spirit.

Dear Lord Jesus,

You made the greatest commitment in history when you left your comfortable throne in heaven to come into this sin-sick world to die in our place. Open my eyes and my heart to the commitment you made to me, so that I will commit to others, especially those in my family. In your name I pray, Amen.

"Place yourselves under each other's authority out of respect for Christ. Wives, place yourselves under your husbands' authority as you have placed yourselves under the Lord's authority. The husband is the head of his wife as Christ is the head of the church. It is his body, and he is its Savior. As the church is under Christ's authority, so wives are under their husbands' authority in everything. Husbands, love your wives as Christ loved the church and gave his life for it. He did this to make the church holy by cleansing it, washing it using water along with spoken words. Then he could present it to himself as a glorious church, without any kind of stain or wrinkle—holy and without faults. So husbands must love their wives as they love their own bodies. A man who loves his wife loves himself. No one ever hated his own body. Instead, he feeds and takes care of it, as Christ takes care of the church. We are parts of his body. That's why a man will leave his father and mother and be united with his wife, and the two will be one. This is a great mystery. (I'm talking about Christ's relationship to the church). But every husband must love his wife as he loves himself, and wives should respect their husbands." *Ephesians 5:21-33*

AFRICAN TIME

SOME YEARS AGO, I TOOK MY FIRST TRIP TO AFRICA as an ex-cop rookie missionary. I rapidly discovered that, no, I had not seen and done it all. "This place is full of all kinds of surprises," I mused.

The Assistant to the Bishop, Martin Shao, and I were doing lunch in the sun on the balcony of the Northern Diocese office of the Lutheran Church of Tanzania. I was busy putting away some delicious chicken and rice, occasionally and cautiously dipping into a wild hot sauce which could also double as an arsonist's accelerant. While juggling spicy food and a fire hose and good conversation with my friend, I watched with watery eyes the market day happenings across the street. From my perch, I could view an open-air African version of Wal-Mart, busy with vendors hawking everything from bananas to baskets. They rolled out their sale items onto thatch mats and haggled loudly with the colorful crowd. It was a flea market with ambience.

"What a great place to be a cop! You just sit at the station drinking coffee and wait for the bad guys to come to you!"

While taking in the scene, I suddenly saw a man break away from the milling shoppers. As quickly as I can tell it, he ran in front of our balcony and up the street. Behind him trailed a mob of obviously irate citizens. The man was making gold-medal time, heroically booking it up the road with his escorts yelling along behind.

"Hey, Martin," I asked, watching the foot pursuit. "What's going on?" "Oh, that," he replied nonchalantly. "That man has probably stolen something at the market. Someone has seen him and now those people from the market are after him." I looked at the impromptu parade with what was now professional interest. I was witnessing a modern African example of the old English, "Hue and Cry" method of law enforcement. Without taking my eyes off the hue-ers and cry-ers, I asked, "So, what will they do if they catch him?" "If those people catch that thief, they will beat him." Martin paused. "They may even kill him."

For a moment, I forgot the fire in my mouth. "So...where's he headed? How does he hope to get away on foot like that?" Martin pointed up the street. "Do you see that building there at the end of the street? That is the police station. The thief is running to the police for protection." He then added with a smile, "This happens all the time. Our thieves would rather go to jail in one piece than remain free and get beaten into many pieces."

Now, in all of my "been there, done that, got the T-shirt" life, it's not often that I do a double-take, but I did one then. After an incredulous pause, I looked at Martin and finally remarked, "What a great place to be a cop! You just sit at the station drinking coffee and wait for the bad guys to come to you!"

As this experience illustrates, Africa is a land of surprises. From these surprises, I learned some lessons that I thought I already knew. Allow me to share those lessons with you, too.

I once had the privilege of preaching at an outdoor service on the slopes of Mt. Kilimanjaro in Tanzania. There were a large number of children in attendance and these kids, some as small as toddlers, all came down to sit on the grass in the front of the audience. There were several preachers who spoke, both before and after me, so I had the opportunity to watch the audience. I was amazed. These children sat quietly and, like the adults, listened—*really* listened—as the preachers spoke. "A preacher's paradise," I thought. It wasn't until later that I figured it out. These kids had no television and no CD players. We, the preachers, were their entertainment, except we were able to actually communicate some spiritual content into their unscrambled minds. The attention span of each child had not been fat-fried by years of fast food commercials.

> **It should be no surprise that we're left at the end of the day wondering why we have no one and nothing left but our rusty toys.**

On my second trip to Africa, I was waiting for an up-country bus in Abidjan, a large city on the French Ivory Coast, on the western side of the continent. There, in a huge open bus stop area covering several city blocks, I struck up a conversation with a man. In my fractured French, I told him that I was there as a missionary. Answering his eager questions, I shared the good news of Jesus Christ and prayed with him. He not only politely allowed this foreigner to talk about spiritual things, but he actually encouraged me to overcome my hesitancy to open up and "impose" my faith on a total stranger. It became plain to me that this man, like many in Africa, could talk about spiritual things in the same way we talk about the weather or the basketball scores. He knew that spiritual matters were just as real as, and certainly more important than, the weather. I could not help but reflect that, if I were to try to engage a stranger here in the United States in conversation about spiritual things, he would probably edge toward the nearest available exit. We are a sensual and materialistic people, often too "civilized" to consider the deeper truths and meanings and relationships of life. It should be no surprise that we're left at the end of the day wondering why we have no one and nothing left but our rusty toys.

In Africa, as in many so-called, "uncivilized" places in the world, age is revered and gray hair is proudly displayed and respectfully observed as a badge of honor and wisdom. In our country, foolish youth is worshipped. We surgically arrange our bodies and color our hair to make ourselves look like our glitzy, but otherwise empty young idols. We do not have the wisdom to appreciate the maturity that experience has given us. We are too shallow to wear our badge of age with dignity and our "civilized" society is too preoccupied with extreme youth to consider how our upside-down attitude is robbing us of one of our greatest potential resources—age. In fact, you'll want to respect the wisdom you see in elderly people.

And, finally, another surprise in Africa. In the United States, we measure civilization by technology and the clock.

In many places like Africa, however, civilization is measured by caring relationships. Thus, in Africa, a person is considered civilized if he takes time to be concerned for others and takes time to have a relationship with God. For example, if a man is walking on a road and meets an elderly acquaintance, he will say something equivalent to, "Hi, how are you?" This question has a different meaning in Africa than it does in America. In our society, this is merely a polite, but superficial greeting. We don't really want to know how a person is doing, because, typically, we are on a schedule and do not have time or interest to listen to an honest and complete answer. We expect the response to be, "I'm fine. How are you?" And, in this way, we can move on to our business at hand. In Africa, though, people will take the time to inquire about your family, your life, and will demonstrate a genuine concern for your welfare. They will often pursue a spiritual life, evidenced by the millions of people coming to God in Africa. God and people, rather than technology and schedules, typically come first.

I do not want to idealize the culture of Africa. There are many problems facing people in that part of the world. I do believe, however, that the surprises to be found in Africa can teach us many things, if we only care to listen. And, I recognize that our circumstances often make it difficult for us to set proper priorities. It is hard to take time to show concern for people when calls are backed up and your caseload is stacked up. Try to remember, though, that to make the most of our lives, sometimes we need to be on "African time." Also, remember that God is always on African time. He always has time for you. He always listens to you. He is always willing to give you the wisdom he has in his Word. He desires nothing more than to show you his love in Jesus Christ. His Son took the time to come to this earth and live as each one of us, so that we can live forever with him in African time. My prayer is that you discover a bit of Africa in your life. Blessings!

Jesus,

When you walked this earth you often took time in your busy schedule to go up on a mountain to talk to your Father in heaven. You took time to care for one sick woman in the crowd. You took time to patiently teach folks who were sometimes pretty dense. You took time with the woman at the well, with Zacchaeus by the road, and with the children in your arms. You took time to wash your disciples' feet. Lord, you never watched the clock, but you sure used your time well. You never—not once—ever let the urgent things interfere with the important things. In your word you remind me that the whole law of God can be summed up simply, "Love God and your neighbor as yourself." You always put your Father and your people first. Help me to do the same,

Amen.

> **In your word you remind me that the whole law of God can be summed up simply, "Love God and your neighbor as yourself."**

HITTING THE WALL

IT WAS SUMMER, 1993. I WAS STANDING IN A BRIGHT and busy airport terminal, but I felt alone and dead in a black universe of depression. I had truly hit The Wall. I couldn't see through it. I couldn't climb over it. I couldn't get around it. I couldn't break through it. I couldn't even see past its dark façade. That façade was now my reality. The only other feeling in my universe was anger. Anger with my circumstances. Anger with myself. Even fist-shaking anger at God for letting me get into this mess.

> **I wasn't sure where that road would take me, but I felt that God would honor my faithfulness.**

In 1988, I quit, in midstream, a successful law enforcement career. I cashed in my retirement, sold my classic '66 Mustang convertible and moved my family from sunny California to Fort Wayne, Indiana to enter Concordia Theological Seminary. I believed I was following God's leading to go into the ministry. I wasn't sure where that road would take me, but I felt that God would honor my faithfulness. Everything would be okay. I also had a great deal of self-confidence, formed through years of achieving my goals as a peace officer. While tipping my hat in God's general direction, I also thought I was very much in control of my life.

My friends in law enforcement were excited about this step. They said, "Hey this is great! You can go to seminary and then come back and minister to us." But, when I got to seminary, I discovered there was no ministry track for law enforcement chaplaincy. If I wanted to minister to peace officers, I would have to do it on my own. And so, even though I was a Fort Wayne Police Department Chaplain and wrote my master's thesis on police chaplaincy, I knew I could not plan on chaplaincy as a goal. I never seriously considered it as a possible full-time ministry. I studied church development instead and helped start two churches in Fort Wayne, Indiana.

> **"Who am I to question this call? I need to trust God and follow Him."**

Then, in my fourth and final year of seminary, our denominational mission board asked me if I would go to West Africa as a missionary. My first reaction was shock. During seminary, I had traveled to Kenya and Tanzania on a brief mission trip, but even though I loved mission work, I had never seriously contemplated going overseas as a missionary. However, I thought, "Who am I to question this call? I need to trust God and follow Him." My wife and I talked and prayed about it with our children, and we decided to go.

For the most part, my cop buddies scratched their heads. One even got angry. He said to me, "What are you doing going to Africa? Your mission board should find someone else. You don't know Africa. You know cops. We're dying out here and you're one of the few who cares and can help us." I told him, "Look, this is my call. I don't have a call to cops. This is the only open door God has given me. I've got to go through it." I was scratching my head, too, but I didn't know what else to do. I figured it was God's job to send me where He wanted. It was my job to go.

We spent a year in Quebec, Canada, studying French, which is the language of the Ivory Coast. During that time, I

We were told we should not go to Africa. I was in shock.

had an opportunity to travel to our new mission field and spent some time with the folks there (mostly refugees from the Liberian civil war). I saw an incredible amount of suffering and also witnessed an incredible hunger for the good news about Jesus Christ. I fell in love with the people there. In the short time I was there, I started two churches, conducted theological training for seventy-five pastor candidates, preached ten times and baptized one hundred and eleven people. Six of the people I baptized spoke French and came forward for baptism after I preached to them in French. They probably worship rocks today because my French was so bad, but when I got back to Quebec, I was definitely fired up and ready to return to Africa.

After completing the remainder of our language study in May of 1993, my family prepared to go overseas. We got our passports and all six of us, including my infant daughter, endured a painful series of shots. We gave away almost every-thing we owned before leaving Canada. We assumed we would buy what we needed in Africa. Then, just like the char-acters in *The Grapes of Wrath*, we loaded up our '83 Buick bomb with our remaining belongings and headed across the country to Colorado Springs, Colorado, where we were sched-uled for some final training. We were due to leave for Africa in a few short weeks. We even had our airline tickets.

Then we hit The Wall. During some final testing, my wife was diagnosed with clinical depression. We were told we should not go to Africa. I was in shock. Here we were in Colorado with little else but the clothes on our backs, driving a car that looked like something I used to check for wants and warrants. We had no home, no furniture, no winter clothes, no plan and no control. My wife was told she couldn't work because of her depression and my salary was not nearly enough to maintain a family of six, not to mention getting started all over again. When we tried to find a place to rent, I found out that displaced missionaries get even less respect than Rodney

> **I was riding a fast freight with no brakes and felt like everyone and every-thing had turned against me.**

Dangerfield. One landlord told us he was worried about our lack of furniture and the potential damage to his carpeting because the baby might "pee on it" while sleeping. I had a good law enforcement career and always made the right moves. I even had a security clearance. What happened? I felt like God wasn't living up to his end of the deal. You know, it's the popular *I'm faithful, therefore God will make everything okay* equation that so many of us choose to believe. I felt that God was jerking my chain and I got angry.

Things went from bad to worse. We had medical bills and we seemed to lack everything. The children were due to start school soon and they had nothing. The one thing we did have was a gold-plated credit rating and I used it big time. Of course, this eventually led to an almost unbearable years-long financial strain, but I felt I had no choice. These and other frustrations piled one on top of another until, finally, I was a basket case. I was riding a fast freight with no brakes and felt like everyone and everything had turned against me. Anger led to the bitterness and depression I felt that day in the airport.

At this point in the story, I should interject that when our friends heard about our move to Colorado Springs, Colorado, they often said, "Hey, Focus on the Family is moving there. Say 'Hello' to Dr. James Dobson for us." (Focus on the Family, the worldwide radio ministry of Dr. James Dobson, is one of America's strongest supporters of families and Christian beliefs and values). My response to these comments was usually, "Yeah, right. Like we're ever going to meet him."

At the airport that day, my wife and I were waiting for our daughter to return from a visit to her grandparents in California. I was lost in a dark fog, feeling crushed by The Wall. At about that same time, our little toddler did her drunk-walk routine over to grab my leg, but just like a good drunk, she lost concentration and started going for the leg of the stranger behind me. My wife looked up from where she was sitting and said, "Steve, look who's standing behind you." I turned around and looked up at a very tall Dr. James Dobson. As it turned out, he and his wife, Shirley, were waiting for their daughter, who happened to be on the same plane as our daughter.

My wife was very excited about meeting Dr. Dobson, but I was in such a funk that I really didn't care. We started a conversation, anyway. I was down so far that, to this day, I don't remember much of our conversation, except that he politely listened to our story and seemed to be a regular guy. Then came the standout moment I *do* remember and will always remember. Dr. Dobson looked at me and asked, "Does God know where you are?"

> **Every day, God continues to pry open my stubborn eyes with the truth that he works in all circumstances, good or bad.**

I wish I could write of all the things that happened after that "divine encounter." Much has been difficult. Much has been good. Our entire family has been affected by past events, but we are doing well. We have experienced a great deal of healing. My wife and I have enjoyed personal successes and we own a nice home with a beautiful view. Like all good materialists, we have filled that home with junk. We've even pulled out of our financial hole. However, all these good things are not the point. This is not a case of God waking up one day, realizing he was slow on the draw and belatedly fixing everything. Rather, it's about me letting go and letting God work The Wall. So, it's time to cut to the chase.

Because I took a detour to Africa, one hundred and eleven people were baptized. Because I hit The Wall, the legitimate needs of my wife and children were met. Because I got stuck in Colorado Springs, I started a church which otherwise would not have been started. Because my train derailed here, my wife found her "dream job." Because I was frustrated in my goals, God gave me a wonderful chaplaincy ministry I never thought possible. The list goes on and on. God has taken every lemon in my life and made, or is making, lemonade. Every day, God continues to pry open my stubborn eyes with the truth that he works in all circumstances, good or bad.

Your story is different from mine, but the principle remains the same. It's not about whether God causes good or bad things to happen to people. Rather, it's about God working his love regardless of The Wall we face. He takes the devil's best shot and fires it back—with interest. The biggest example of this is Jesus on the cross. God took Satan's biggest victory, the death of Jesus, and turned it into the devil's greatest defeat, our salvation.

I know I will face The Wall again in the future, but I'll take my chances with God. It's really no chance at all. He has never let me down. He will never let you down. It's The Wall that doesn't stand a chance.

God,

Sometimes I hit a wall that I can't seem to get around or under or over or through...(tell him about the walls in your life). Help me to understand that these obstacles in my path are really opportunities to grow my faith. By the power of your promises, help me leap over each and every one. Thanks!

Amen.

> "For by Thee I have run through a troop; and by my God have I leaped over a wall." Psalm 18:29

THE FIVE
GOLDEN KEYS OF
STRESS MANAGEMENT
FOR COPS

DOCTOR BERNADINE HEALY, FORMER DEAN OF THE College of Medicine and Public Health at Ohio State University, spoke in 1998 at the FBI National Academy Associates National Conference. In her excellent presentation, she observed that there are five keys we must have to effectively manage stress:

1. Control

2. Predictability

3. Outlet for Frustration

4. Social Contacts

5. Optimism (Hope)

As I listened to Dr. Healy, I realized that, because of the demands and pressures of law enforcement, each of these keys is problematic for peace officers. These keys can bring baggage that, unfortunately, *add* to your stress.

Control. Peace officers must exert effective control. You must have "command presence." You are in a daily battle for control, but, ironically, your work thrusts you into many circumstances that are beyond your control. This lack of control by a person highly trained to exercise it is a source of never-ending frustration and stress. This is made worse when that command presence carries over into your personal life. Family and friends do not appreciate being controlled, and I'm sure they do not hesitate to let you know that fact.

Second, there is very little that is *predictable* in law enforcement. Part of the attraction for people entering into the law enforcement field is the excitement of that unpredictability. This "need for speed" can turn an officer into an adrenaline junkie and can eventually cause stress-related physiological, emotional, and even spiritual problems. Dr. Jekyll excitement transforms into Mr. Hyde stress.

When searching for an *outlet for frustration*, peace officers sometimes get trapped into attractive, but unhealthy outlets, which only adds to your stress. For example, a traditional outlet (which has nothing to do with church!), is "choir practice," when officers gather after work to drink and relax. You may self-medicate with a depressant (alcohol) to come down from your work-related adrenaline high. Aided by alcohol, you're then able to let down your guard with empathetic fellow officers. This often translates into what is effectively a drug-enabled group therapy session—without the therapy. Toss in some sexual or other misadventures, and you may wind up holding a ticking time bomb that can eventually blow up in your face in the form of alcoholism, divorce, estranged families, sexually transmitted diseases, work-related problems, etc.

Social contacts. An officer's work tends to drive a wedge between him or her and the broader community. For instance, if an officer is at a social function and tells someone what he does, that person may "dump" on him about a traffic ticket. After a while, the officer may duck any social contact, except with fellow officers. As another example, a female officer may date a man, only to discover that he is either intimidated or attracted by the fact that she carries a gun, and thus does not relate to her in a normal way.

> **Part of the attraction for people entering into the law enforcement field is the excitement of that unpredictability.**

And, finally, *hope* as a stress management tool is hard to come by for peace officers. You see the worst side of life. You are not called on duty to attend a tea party—unless maybe a drunk disrupts it. Without a world view, a positive belief system, to give you hope in the midst of unremitting evil and tragedy, officers are doomed to despair.

You may wonder if there are *any* effective means of stress management for peace officers. I'm happy to say that, with a strong spiritual foundation you will find the "golden keys" that are specifically effective for peace officers. Let's look at each of the five stress busters again from a spiritual perspective:

Golden Key #1: God is in control. Much of the *control* you appear to have is illusory. With time and experience, many officers come to this potentially demoralizing conclusion. We simply can't be in control of everything. However, while there are many things that are simply outside our control, we can trust our loving God for each of them. We often do not understand the "why?" or "what?" or "how?" of life, but we can know the "who?" That person is God, who reveals himself in the pages of the Bible and in the life of our Lord and Savior Jesus Christ. As God of the universe, he is truly in control. In a happy irony, when we yield to him and trust him, we gain control of our lives in undreamed of ways and can ultimately deal with any stress—even the stress of death.

> **As God of the universe, he is truly in control.**

Golden Key #2: God's promises are predictable. Although little of our work is *predictable*, the promises of God restore predictability in all avenues of our lives. We may still struggle with the daily crises of life, but in the light of God's Word we can be sure of the process and sure of the outcome.

Golden Key #3: Faith overcomes frustration. When searching for an *outlet for frustration*, Christian officers know that, first and foremost, faith cannot be placed in people or circumstances, but only in God. This realization alone will prevent much of the stress you face. Stress is reduced with a healthy, balanced life, including a spiritual life of prayer, study of the Bible and warm and nurturing Christian fellowship, all of which give a positive alternative to outlets such as "choir practice." Your prayers don't have to be complicated or fancy (in fact, they may be offered to God at any moment, using the most simple words, such as "Help me, God, I'm not sure what's going down here.") You may want to study the Bible with other Christians or with a Bible study reference book. Let me also give you some practical advice that "saved my bacon" when I was an officer—stay mutually close and accountable with a fellow officer who is a believing Christian and *listen*.

Golden Key #4: Connect to, and through, the Christian church. Healthy *social contacts* for a Christian peace officer can be found in any church that honors God's law and addresses sin and sorrow with the free grace of God in Christ. Otherwise, it will be a hotbed of hypocrisy—more burden than blessing to already overburdened officers. We need a spiritual family that—while imperfect like us—will love, forgive, accept and encourage us according to God's Word. And, what about that neighbor or acquaintance who doesn't seem to relate to you? Before you isolate yourself by socializing only with other officers or even church members, remember that God also calls us to be the light of the world. Take a few minutes to chat with your child's teacher at the grocery store. Go to the neighborhood block party you've been avoiding every year. Do these simple things to stretch yourself experientially and to give of yourself. Invest yourself just a bit into the lives

> We need a spiritual family that—while imperfect like us—will love, forgive, accept and encourage us according to God's Word.

of others and you may be surprised at the number of people who would actually like to share your sports interests, hobbies and jokes. More importantly, you'll be blessed by God as you're bringing God's blessing to others.

Golden Key #5: Hold on to hope. Finally, we come to *hope*. Here we conclude with an exhortation and promise from God's Word, "Let us hold unswervingly to the hope we profess, for He who promised is faithful." (Hebrews 10:23). You can count on God's promises in your life, so don't ever, ever let go of your hope in him.

I pray you put to good use the "five golden keys" of stress management every day.

Lord,

You and I both know this old world isn't getting any better and so, if I look to better circumstances or depend upon other people for my own stress-free peace and happiness, I've got a longer wait and more frustration than on an L.A. freeway at rush hour. No...if I'm going to have peace and joy, it can't come from the outside in, it must come from the inside out. The problem is that some days I feel like I'm running on empty. I need you to top me off to overflowing with your Spirit. Please...fill my heart. Fill me with your strength, your joy, your peace, your hope, and your love. In the stress-filled deserts of this life, let your joy flow through me like cool water from a spring. In Jesus' name I pray,

Amen.

ONE MORE

God provides the power for us to become Christians.
God encourages us to spend time with Him on a regular basis.
God wants us to spend time with other Christians.
God calls us to study His Word and grow as Christians.
God asks us to allow Him into our hearts.

You may have some pretty compelling reasons for avoiding God. You may say, "I don't want to go to a church full of hypocrites." You may think you have everything under control. You may not want to face the reality of your life when you face God. You may use the perfect excuse, "I have no extra time," when it's time to face God. You can probably think up much more inventive and effective excuses than these.

> **You may use the perfect excuse, "I have no extra time," when it's time to face God.**

The truth is, despite our excuses and despite our attempts at avoiding God, he stands waiting for you. His love isn't limited and it's never too late, no matter what you've done or where you've been in this life. There's always room for one more. There's always room for you.

Lord,

All excuses aside, if I'm honest I have to admit that sometimes it's simply my sin that gets in the way of my walk with you. Other times I find an empty hole where my heart should be and so I have no strength or even desire to follow you...(here give him your specific sins and sorrows). So, Lord, my prayer is the same as King David's in Psalm 51, "Create a clean heart in me, O God, and renew a faithful spirit within me. Do not force me away from your presence and do not take your Holy Spirit from me. Restore the joy of your salvation to me, and provide me with a spirit of willing obedience,"

Amen.

> **I don't look back, I lengthen my stride, and I run straight toward the goal to win the prize that God's heavenly call offers in Christ Jesus."**

"It's not that I've already reached the goal or have already completed the course. But I run to win that which Jesus Christ has already won for me. Brothers and sisters, I can't consider myself a winner yet. This is what I do: I don't look back, I lengthen my stride, and I run straight toward the goal to win the prize that God's heavenly call offers in Christ Jesus." *Philippians 3:12-14*

THE BASICS OF BELIEF:
TYING IT ALL TOGETHER

YOU MAY WONDER WHAT THE MESSAGE OF CHRIST is all about. And, if you're like many of us, you may be unsure about the Bible, prayer and "eternal life." So, let's take a look at some of the basic elements of Christian belief to put the pieces of the puzzle together.

The Bible, also called the "Scriptures," "Scripture," or the "Word of God," was humanly written, but inspired by the Spirit of God. So, this "Word" empowers us both to faith and life. There are sixty-six "books" of the Bible. They were written by many different human writers over a period of about 1,600 years, from about 1500 B.C. to about 100 A.D. Because they were divinely inspired (which means that God is the author of the Word), they show a remarkable consistency. The Word of God itself tells us its purpose and how we should read it. So, its message is the same to all, if we humbly listen in faith to what God's Word says.

The main purpose of the Bible is to tell us the true story of God's grace (undeserved love). This grace was given to us in the gift of his Son, our Lord and Savior Jesus Christ. "Lord" means "Master." "Savior" means he saved us from our sins and freely gives us eternal life. "Jesus" is the human name of our Lord and means, "God Saves." "Christ" is another word for "Messiah," and means "God's Anointed One." This refers to Jesus' role as God's promised Savior of the world.

Because Jesus is God's one and only Son, he is true God Himself. Because Jesus was born by God of the Virgin Mary, he is also true man. Only as a true man could he die on the cross to take upon himself the punishment we deserved for our rebellion against God. Only as true God could he take away the sins of the whole world by his redeeming death. "Redeem" means "to buy back." In this case, it means that God bought back his helpless children from the clutches of sin and Satan by the blood of Jesus. So, Jesus is also referred to as our Redeemer. We are God's children twice, first by creation, and then again by redemption.

> **Most of all, God's Word tells the true story of history's ultimate Peace Officer, Jesus Christ, who laid down his life "to protect and serve" the entire world, including peace officers.**

Our eternal life depends upon the grace, the undeserved kindness, of God alone, received through faith alone, as revealed by the Spirit of God through the Scripture alone.

The Bible addresses in detail humanity's sinful and suffering state, a state that peace officers observe every day and which requires their constant presence. It affects them, too.

God's Word lays the foundation for the law that officers serve. It outlines the importance, the authority and the mission of law enforcement. It tells real-life stories of cops—stories which have modern-day applications. It provides spiritual protection, promises, power and peace in the face of temptation, trial and trouble. God's Word speaks to our situation as husbands, wives, fathers, mothers, friends, "sinner-saints," and on and on. Most of all, God's Word tells the true story of history's ultimate Peace Officer, Jesus Christ, who laid down his life "to protect and serve" the entire world, including peace officers (2 Timothy 3:14-17).

God's law is perfect. So, too, is his love. In his great love, he has given us the way of life. He sent his Son, Jesus Christ, who took on himself the death sentence we deserved. In him, we have certain hope of eternal life (Titus 1:1-2). He is the great Peace Officer—our "Good Shepherd" (Psalm 23, John 10:1-18).

> **The message of Christianity found in God's Word is unique in all the world.**

In God's Word, Jesus says, "I am the way, the truth and the life. No one goes to the Father except through me." (John 14:6). We should not regard Jesus' claim as unreasonable or too exclusive. His are the words and actions of a rescuer who carries us from the fire through the one door of escape. A person trapped by the flames will not think the one way of escape is too narrow or too narrow-minded. That person will instead gladly be rescued by that one way, and will, furthermore, be eternally grateful to the rescuer.

The entire world, because of our imperfection outside of Jesus Christ, has been kidnapped and is held hostage by Satan in the world of sin and sorrow. There is no escape from that truth. No self-righteousness, no other faith, no religious or moral or civil "good" works, no philosophy, no psychology, and nothing and no one else will save us except our Savior. Inadequate human ideas shout out the self-help slogan, "Do good and feel good!" But, the Word of God tells us that Jesus Christ, our one Savior, conducted the greatest hostage rescue of history by gathering us each in his arms and announcing, "It's already done!" (Romans 5:6-11). You see, Jesus paid that ransom for us, and the price didn't come cheap.

> **Praying is simply talking to God in faith.**

The message of Christianity found in God's Word is unique in all the world. This message proclaims that, because of what Jesus sacrificed on the cross, we have the free gift of eternal life. It's ours by faith, not by any act of good. We need to go his way. We need to listen to his truth. We need to receive his life.

So, how do we survive on our spiritual beat? We need a saving relationship with God. Our relationship with God does not depend on us, because we are not perfect and we often fail even though we believe. Our relationship with God is based completely on the free gift of life which Christ has already won for us through his death and resurrection. By the power of the Holy Spirit, we turn to Christ from sin, to trust him and obey him daily.

Praying is simply talking to God in faith. Right now, I invite you to respond to God's Word with this prayer and receive God's peace.

Father in heaven,

I confess to you with sorrow and sadness that I have failed to keep your perfect law. I have fallen victim to sin, Satan and myself. I humbly come before You, in faith, to ask Your forgiveness. I confess that I cannot rescue myself, but instead rely completely on the backup of your Son, Jesus Christ, who took my sentence of death and died on the cross for me. In that heroic act of love, he arrested Satan and took away my sins. Thank you that, because of Christ's resurrection, I, too, will live forever. Because of Your great love for me, I turn from my own way to trust and obey Christ by the power of Your Holy Spirit. Jesus, my Peace Officer, renew me. Come back me up and patrol my heart and life. Protect and serve me forever in your peace and help me to always be your peace officer,

Amen.

Stephen C. Lee

WHAT LEGACY WILL YOU LEAVE?

I T'S CALLED THE QUARTER CIRCLE AND IT'S ON HIGHWAY 50 at the east end of Gunnison, Colorado. It's not fancy, but the folks at this restaurant serve up a friendly small-town feeling along with good, homestyle cooking. And, as my wife and I found on the way to our breakfast table, they

> **Grandma was the sun around which our family revolved.**

also serve up good local artwork. We were about to discover an unexpected vacation treat.

We saw a variety of pencil prints on the walls, mostly cowboys and horses and western scenes. But, hanging on the wall above our table was a different kind of print. Created by the same artist, in the same style, it showed an eye-catching profile of wrinkled old hands pressed together in prayer. Also, more compelling, they tenderly cupped the bowed head of a small child, who, eyes closed, was resting in them, its own small hands folded in tiny imitation atop the aged ones. The print was a portrait of one generation's legacy of faith, hope, and love to another.

My wife couldn't take her eyes off the picture. "I love it!" she exclaimed. "Those look like your Grandma's hands." My

Grandma's hands. I remembered those hands from when I, too, was a child and, yes, they did look like the hands in the picture. Grandma Anna was short, wrinkled, and walked with a stooped arthritic shuffle. She was also one of the most beautiful women I've ever met. Like Anna in the Bible (Luke 2:36-38), her beauty came from the heart.

How could this woman say those things? How could she keep her love, her faith, her hope, and her joy through so many hard times?

Grandma had a hard life. She was born in poverty in Minnesota. Her father died when she was a baby. Her mother was deaf and needed care. Her first husband abandoned her and the children. She remarried to a man who suffered from emphysema. She suffered through the Depression, trying to provide for her large family. Later, because of unfortunate circumstances, she willingly raised some of her grandchildren, even while caring for her sick husband and suffering from her own rheumatism. These are but a few of the things Grandma endured in her life. It seems she never got a break and, by human right and reason, should have become bitter.

And, yet, some of the happiest times I ever had as a child were spent at her humble house. Grandma was the sun around which our family revolved. Not that she was the center of attention, but she *was* the center of attraction. The gravity of her love drew us into orbit around her, especially at holiday time. She loved her family and always sought to give us her best in every way. She had a servant's heart. She had the heart of Jesus.

As I looked at the print on the wall, I remembered back to the time before Grandma died, before my wife and I were married. I had just introduced them to each other as we met to go into a restaurant, and Grandma took my fiancée's arm to steady herself. As it turned out, Grandma steadied my wife-to-be instead. Most people stick to petty conversation when they first meet. Not Grandma. She cut to the chase, as if the world could end at any moment and the most important things had to be said *now*. She lovingly wrapped my fiancée's smooth, young hands in her wrinkled, old ones, looked her in the eyes, and said, "Have faith, girl. I've trusted Jesus all my life and he's never failed me." At that moment, my future wife fell in love with Grandma and, from then on, followed her around like a puppy.

When I heard Grandma say those words, I was not surprised at the time, because I knew her and they reflected perfectly who she was. Years later, however, the memory of her words moved me to awe. How could this woman say those things? How could she keep her love, her faith, her hope, and her joy through so many hard times? How could she, in her poverty, deliver such riches to her family, more than any earthly wealth could ever buy? Where did she mine such gold that never failed, despite an endlessly difficult life?

Before we can answer these questions, we first need an illustration. My mom always said that it wasn't just Dad's South Pacific tan that won her heart after World War II. She saw how lovingly he treated Grandma and correctly figured he would treat her in the same way. Dad, for his part, saw that, in addition to being friendly and cute, my Mom was a great cook and was good with children. I suppose these were all politically incorrect reasons for marriage, but they were good enough to provide a happy 50th anniversary celebration years later. But, here's the point: Grandma was a key player in making my Dad and Mom's marriage and family a success. She loved her son. He, in turn, loved his mom. My Mom saw that love and fell in love with Dad. Dad, because he had been loved by Grandma and understood love, loved Mom. We kids saw Dad and Mom's love and grew up secure and happy. End of story? End of legacy? No, not even now…

I have known many officers over the years. I remember the many gods they, and I, too, as an officer, sometimes chased: adrenaline, fame, power, promotion, etc. How many of those gods give a final gift to write home about? How many of those leave a legacy that blesses the generations to follow? I once heard an officer comment, "Wives come and go, but you have only one career." Not surprisingly, his life was a wreck.

Most cops enter law enforcement with the idea that they want to help people and make a positive difference. In the real world, they discover that, instead of them rolling over the world, the world often rolls over them. Many people don't want to be helped. Many people don't care. Many people never even notice when a cop's obituary is posted and, even among fellow officers, a cop can be quickly forgotten.

I remembered my Grandma again. She made a greater impact than most, simply by giving Jesus' love to the family and friends that God had given her. She left a lasting legacy.

My wife wanted the print because she loved it. I wanted to give her the print because we were on vacation and it was our 21st wedding anniversary. We both took it home to remember what counts. Now, I ask you, "What legacy will *you* leave?"

May God always bless you and back you up on life's beat!

∞

ABOUT CHAPLAIN STEVE LEE

STEVE LEE IS A FORMER CALIFORNIA PEACE OFFICER with many years of experience. He worked in a variety of roles during his law enforcement career: Police officer (patrol, juvenile officer), sheriff's deputy and sergeant (jail, patrol, deputy coroner, SWAT, investigations), and federal special agent (major crimes, foreign counter-intelligence).

Chaplain Lee left law enforcement in 1988 to attend Concordia Theological Seminary in Fort Wayne, Indiana, and has since served as a pastor and law enforcement chaplain. He has been called by Shepherd of the Hills Lutheran Church to serve as full-time Executive Director of Peace Officer Ministries, Inc., which he founded in 1996.

Steve Lee serves as a chaplain for the Colorado Springs Police Department and for the U.S. Bureau of Alcohol, Tobacco and Firearms. He is a member in good standing of the International Conference of Police Chaplains (ICPC), where he has attained his Master Chaplaincy certification.

Chaplain Lee holds an Associates degree in Law Enforcement, a Bachelors degree in Psychology and a Masters of Divinity degree from Concordia Theological Seminary. He is married and has four children. He resides in Colorado Springs, Colorado.

ABOUT PEACE OFFICER MINISTRIES

PEACE OFFICER MINISTRIES, INC. IS A NATIONAL
Christian law enforcement chaplaincy ministry that provides direct help during times of trouble. Peace Officer
Ministries also serves as a chaplaincy resource for officers,
chaplains, police agencies, churches, and communities. We
provide consulting, training, and written materials, including
a Bible for officers.

Our Mission: In keeping with our Lord's Great
Commission, Peace Officer Ministries brings the saving and
strengthening Gospel of Jesus Christ to as many as possible,
and especially to peace officers and their families, through law
enforcement chaplaincy (Matthew 28:19-20).

Our Means: We believe that the Bible is the only author-
itative and life-giving Word of God. Its truths form the foundation upon which we minister (2 Timothy 3:14-17).

Our Motive: Peace officers are God's servants, through
whom he maintains law and order in society. We all have a
duty to honor and support peace officers (Romans 13:1-7).
Christians have an additional motive for serving those who
protect and serve us, because the love of Christ compels us to
be his ambassadors to everyone (2 Corinthians 5:14-21).

Officers, and those with whom they work, are deeply
affected by mankind's failure to keep the law of God. Because
of their exposure to this failure and its consequences, officers
are especially at high risk. The law is good, but because of our
sinful nature, it is powerless to overcome sin and death. The
law fails as the source of spiritual life. Because of this, all

people, including peace officers and those with whom they work, need the healing and nurturing of Christ (Romans 8:3).

Our Method: We strive for professional competence and evangelical excellence. We practice pastoral commitment, consistency, and confidentiality (2 Timothy 4:1-2). We only serve when and where we are invited (1 Peter 3:15b-16a). We serve everyone without discrimination (John 3:16), and make referrals when appropriate. We always strive to serve within the law and law enforcement agency guidelines. We seek to be gracious to all, including those who disagree with our beliefs. We do not compete with the ministry of the local church, but always seek to serve it. The development of law enforcement chaplaincy everywhere is a chief goal of our work.

For information about Peace Officer Ministries, or to receive our free monthly ministry letter, contact:

Peace Officer Ministries
P.O. Box 63177
Colorado Springs, CO 80962
Toll free (877)-487-1717
Website: www.peaceofficerministries.org
Email: peaceofficermin@earthlink.net